T0318498

Cambridge Elements ☰

Elements in Child Development
edited by
Marc H. Bornstein
*Eunice Kennedy Shriver National Institute of Child Health and Human
Development, Bethesda
Institute for Fiscal Studies, London
UNICEF, New York City*

CHILDREN AND CLIMATE CHANGE

Ann V. Sanson
University of Melbourne

Karina V. Padilla Malca
The University of Edinburgh

Judith L. Van Hoorn
University of the Pacific

Susie E.L. Burke
University of Queensland

CAMBRIDGE
UNIVERSITY PRESS

Shaftesbury Road, Cambridge CB2 8EA, United Kingdom

One Liberty Plaza, 20th Floor, New York, NY 10006, USA

477 Williamstown Road, Port Melbourne, VIC 3207, Australia

314–321, 3rd Floor, Plot 3, Splendor Forum, Jasola District Centre, New Delhi – 110025, India

103 Penang Road, #05–06/07, Visioncrest Commercial, Singapore 238467

Cambridge University Press is part of Cambridge University Press & Assessment, a department of the University of Cambridge.

We share the University's mission to contribute to society through the pursuit of education, learning and research at the highest international levels of excellence.

www.cambridge.org
Information on this title: www.cambridge.org/9781009114950

DOI: 10.1017/9781009118705

First published 2022

A catalogue record for this publication is available from the British Library.

ISBN 978-1-009-11495-0 Paperback
ISSN 2632-9948 (online)
ISSN 2632-993X (print)

Children and Climate Change

Elements in Child Development

DOI: 10.1017/9781009118705
First published online: August 2022

Ann V. Sanson
University of Melbourne

Karina V. Padilla Malca
The University of Edinburgh

Judith L. Van Hoorn
University of the Pacific

Susie E.L. Burke
University of Queensland

Author for correspondence: Ann V. Sanson, annvs@unimelb.edu.au

Abstract: The existential threat posed by climate change presents a challenge to all those concerned about the next generation. This Element reviews and discusses its implications for the development of children (ages zero to twelve) today and in the future, and for the parents, teachers, researchers, and professionals who have responsibility for children. This Element adopts a bioecological model to examine both the direct impacts on children's physical and psychological well-being and indirect impacts through all the systems external to the child, emphasising the greater vulnerability of children in the Global South. Given the evidence of well-founded climate anxiety, this Element examines children's coping strategies and discusses the key roles of caregivers and schools in protecting and preparing children to face current and future challenges – with knowledge, hope, and agency as central themes. This Element highlights many under-researched areas and calls for action by all those caring for and about children's future.

This Element also has a video abstract: www.cambridge.org/
ChildDevelopment_Sanson_abstract

Keywords: climate change, children, climate impacts, child coping and support, child development

ISBNs: 9781009114950 (PB), 9781009118705 (OC)
ISSNs: 2632-9948 (online), 2632-993X (print)

Contents

1 Introduction and Overview

Climate change poses an existential threat to children unlike any that previous generations have had to face. Wars, economic depressions, and pandemics may have terrible impacts on children but they do not risk the total collapse of civilisation and biodiversity. This Element seeks to review and discuss the implications of the climate crisis for the development of children today and in the future.

1.1 The Climate Crisis

There is now no reasonable doubt that climate change is happening, is caused by human behaviour, and will have catastrophic consequences without urgent action. The latest report from the Intergovernmental Panel on Climate Change (IPCC, 2021) provides the clearest picture yet of the past, present, and future climate and documents how global temperatures have risen in response to rising greenhouse gas concentrations. Levels of carbon dioxide (CO_2) are now higher than they have been for four to five million years, at which time sea levels were 10–20 metres higher than currently and trees were growing in Antarctica (Steffen et al., 2016).

The IPCC (2021) report reflects major advances in the science of attribution[1] and concludes that climate change is now a causal factor in most extreme weather events. At the time of writing, the global temperature rise is about 1.1 degrees Celsius (°C) above pre-industrial levels (Steffen et al., 2016). Even this level of warming has made the world too hot, as shown by the record-breaking heatwaves, wildfires, hurricanes, droughts, flooding, and coastal inundation that have become commonplace. Some coastal and island populations have been forced to relocate, and extreme temperatures, droughts, reduced crop yields, and water shortages are leading to mass migrations and contributing to intrastate and interstate conflict and refugee crises. Climate scientists are also increasing their understanding of complex feedback loops and chains of events causing further climate disruption. For example, melting of the permafrost in the Arctic releases large amounts of methane, a potent greenhouse gas (Gray, 2018), and Arctic warming is likely to start a chain of processes that will ultimately result in periods of extreme cold in northern mid-latitudes such as the USA (Cohen et al., 2021).

The United Nations (UN) Secretary-General António Guterres described the IPCC report as nothing less than 'a code red for humanity – the alarm bells are deafening, and the evidence is irrefutable' (UN, 2021a, para. 2). The report warns that, unless there are immediate, rapid, and large-scale reductions in greenhouse gas emissions, limiting warming to close to 1.5°C or even 2°C will

---

[1] Attribution science addresses the role of climate change in specific weather and climate events.

be beyond reach. To have a chance to avoid worse impacts, global greenhouse gas emissions need to be halved by 2030, and cut to zero by 2050, at the same time as drawing down excess gases already present in the atmosphere. Furthermore, climate scientists warn that the Earth is close to irreversible tipping points; for example, changes in ocean currents, which would have catastrophic impacts (Steffen et al., 2018). However, as of early 2022, most countries are not on track to meet these targets (UN, 2021b).

Even with the transformative action that is needed to stay within safe limits, it could take twenty to thirty years for global temperatures to stabilise. In the 2020s and beyond, increasing climate impacts are predicted across the world, including more intense rainfall and associated flooding as well as more intense droughts in many regions; continued sea-level rises; amplified permafrost thawing, loss of seasonal snow cover, melting of glaciers and ice sheets, and loss of summer Arctic sea ice; and ocean warming, with more frequent marine heatwaves, ocean acidification, and reduced oxygen levels (IPCC, 2021). In addition, climate change is contributing to the threatened extinction of around one million species of animals and plants (Intergovernmental Science-Policy Platform on Biodiversity and Ecosystem Services (IPBES), 2019).

Climate change is a global phenomenon, but it is important to recognise significant disparities in the scale of its impacts. Despite greenhouse gases being emitted predominantly in the Global North,[2] their impacts are and will continue to be felt most severely in the Global South.[3] However, the capacity to prevent, prepare for, adapt to, and respond to these impacts is typically weaker in countries in the Global South (Hanna & Oliva, 2016). Climate change also has direct detrimental and inequitable impacts on Indigenous peoples around the world, disproportionately threatening their self-determination and their human rights to land, health, water, food, housing, and life itself.

An even starker inequity is that current and future generations of children will suffer disproportionately, even though they are not responsible for the emissions. As discussed in more detail in Section 2, the World Health Organization estimates that over 80 per cent of the physical health impacts of climate change will be experienced by children (McMichael, 2014). Roughly 85 per cent of the world's children live in the Global South, and the combination of age and location makes these children doubly vulnerable (United Nations Children's Fund (UNICEF), 2014). Climate change can thus be considered an issue of

---

[2] Also referred to as high-income countries, the developed world, the minority world, or the WEIRD (Western, educated, industrialized, rich democracies) world, comprising approximately 12 per cent of the world's population.

[3] Also referred to as low- and middle-income countries, the developing world, or the majority world.

structural violence, intergenerational injustice, and a violation of children's rights (Sanson & Burke, 2019; UNICEF, 2021a), with profound developmental implications.

The consequences of climate change for today's generation of children were clearly demonstrated by Thiery and colleagues (2021). Based on careful modelling, they showed how children born in 2020 will fare in comparison to people born in 1960 under three scenarios: (a) if climate action is limited to global pledges made in 2021; (b) if action is taken to limit warming to 2°C; and (c) if action is taken to limit warming to 1.5°C. They estimated that, under scenarios a, b, and c, respectively, today's children will experience seven, six, or four times as many heatwaves in their lives than children born in 1960. Similar or stronger results were found for six other types of extreme climate-related events (wildfires, crop failures, droughts, river floods, heatwaves, and tropical cyclones). There were strong variations by region (with the Middle East and North Africa worst impacted) and by income category (with greatest effects in low-income countries, which also have the most children). Thiery and colleagues (2021) noted that their results likely underestimated the intergenerational inequities because they did not consider compound (co-occurring) events, some types of climate-induced events such as coastal flooding, and indirect effects such as destruction of schooling infrastructure and forced migration that may have lifelong impacts. They concluded that while limiting warming to 1.5°C would substantially reduce the burden on children, it would still leave the next generation with unprecedented exposure to extreme weather events.

In the face of this existential crisis, why is humanity so slow to act? While the exploitative patterns of behaviour that have led to the crisis and the lack of action to address it often have their roots in philosophical, religious, political, and economic belief systems (see Newell et al., 2022; Wiseman, 2021), there are also many psychological factors that inhibit action on climate change (Australian Psychological Society (APS), 2017; Gifford, 2011). Some people still perceive climate change as something happening 'elsewhere' or 'in the future', not here and now, despite the ubiquitous evidence of its impacts. Some people wish to maintain the status quo, believing that things can continue to be as they are now (termed 'system justification') – these include those with vested interests in 'business as usual' and short-term profits, such as those involved in the fossil fuel industry. A small but influential number of people, some of whom are influenced and/or funded by the fossil fuel industry, still claim to deny the reality of climate change. Many others are resistant to change and experience discomfort and fear when contemplating the changes in lifestyles that might be involved in transitioning to a zero-carbon economy. For many, the natural desire to avoid emotional distress leads to avoidance of contemplating the reality of climate change and the havoc it threatens to wreak on human life, which inevitably arouses distressing feelings. Finally, many people may understand the threat of climate change but feel powerless to do anything about it. When exploring how climate change impacts the development of the next generation, and how young people can best be supported in this context, it is important to consider how factors such as these – perceived distance in time and space, resistance to change, reluctance to confront uncomfortable feelings, and a sense of helplessness – may affect the responses of both children and those adults with responsibility for their care and development.

As this summary of the stark reality of the climate crisis implies, reviewing and discussing its implications for the children of today and tomorrow is no simple undertaking. First, the range of climate impacts is large and diverse, varies across contexts, and plays out over time. Second, we do not yet know if the world's governments will rise to the challenge and commit to the urgent, whole-of-economy large-scale transformative actions that are needed to limit global warming to 1.5°C. As a result, the extent of future impacts is currently unknowable – they could theoretically be minimal (although no current modelling predicts this) or involve widespread upheaval and suffering in the context of an unstable climate and rapid societal change, or billions of deaths, ecosystem collapse, and even the collapse of human civilisation. Third, climate change affects all aspects of children's development – physical, cognitive, social, behavioural, and emotional. Fourth and critically, despite the seriousness of the issues involved, researchers have been very slow to address climate impacts on children's development, especially for children aged from birth to twelve years who are the focus of this Element. This is even more true of children from the Global South. The body of research specifically addressing climate change and children's development is thus small and incomplete. We therefore rely on research on particular slow-moving climate-related changes and more sudden extreme weather events, reports from governmental, intergovernmental, and non-governmental organisations (NGOs), and on developmental theory, to draw together existing knowledge and develop recommendations for future directions.

Overview of Subsequent Sections

In the following sections, we review the research evidence on how children's development and well-being are affected by climate change and what is needed to protect them. We adopt a broad bioecological model of development (informed by Bronfenbrenner & Morris, 2006; Tudge, 2008), recognising that children's development occurs, over time, through interactions between themselves and their environmental contexts – in contrast with the view of children as passive 'one-way' recipients of the actions and influences of others. Tudge (2008) captured these interdependent interactions with the phrase 'synergetic interplay', taking into account these interactive processes, the child, the context, and time – because climate change is explicitly about change over time.

Throughout this Element, we draw on the bioecological model to discuss the implications of climate change for children. We therefore consider children's own individual characteristics and direct interactions with microsystems such as family, friends, and school, and the interactions between these microsystems (mesosystems) and the other systems external to these proximal systems. The latter include their parents' workplaces and the community in which they live (exosystem) and the large, distal macrosystems (such as the physical environment, cultural factors, and government policies) that influence children and their microsystems indirectly. Because human development cannot be separated from the physical environmental contexts in which it takes place, we view climate change as a macrosystem phenomenon that is occurring over time and examine how it is manifested at different levels of the child's ecology, with direct and indirect impacts on children's well-being, and their physical, emotional, social, and cognitive development. Figure 1 shows the bioecological model we adopt, as developed by Tudge (2008).

Our focus is on childhood (ages zero to twelve years), but we also look back to the prenatal period and forward to adolescence and adulthood. This broader time frame allows us to gain a fuller picture of the impacts of climate change on

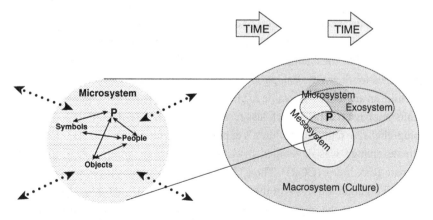

Figure 1 Visual representation of the PPCT model of Urie Bronfenbrenner's bioecological theory, showing the active Person (P) engaging in proximal Processes (P) with people, symbols, and objects in a microsystem in interaction with other Contexts (C) involving both change and continuity over Time (T) (from Tudge, 2008; used with permission from Cambridge University Press)

the growing individual and to consider the ways in which children's experiences early in life may affect their future development. Furthermore, it allows us to consider how children can be supported now to enable them to thrive in the future that awaits them.

We start by reviewing how exposure to gradual climate changes, such as changes in rainfall patterns, sea-level rise, and droughts, and to the sudden extreme weather events that are becoming more frequent and intense as a result of climate change (e.g., floods, hurricanes, wildfires) are related to children's health, development, and well-being (Section 2). We then turn to how children's awareness of the threat posed by climate change affects their emotional well-being, with evidence that many children globally are expressing fear and anxiety about their perceived future lives (Section 3). Section 4 provides a discussion of effective coping strategies for children, where senses of self-efficacy and agency emerge as important protective factors. Sections 5 and 6 then explore the roles of parents and educational settings, respectively, in supporting children. We next consider the skills and attributes that the next generation of children will need in the longer term to cope with the climate-induced changes that they are going to experience in the world they will inherit (Section 7). Finally, Section 8 draws these learnings together, identifies the many gaps in current knowledge, and examines the implications for professionals with responsibilities for this and future generations of children, ending with a call to action for all of us.

2 Impacts of Exposure to Climate-Related Events on Children's Health, Development, and Well-Being

This section discusses the impacts of climate change on the well-being of children, applying the bioecological model (see Figure 1) to understand how the interactions of children with their families, communities, and societies create and reinforce challenges for their physical, psychological, and social development.

Children are more vulnerable to climate change impacts than adolescents and adults but have received much less research focus (Burke et al., 2018). The first comprehensive report on children's exposure and vulnerability to the impacts of climate change was developed by UNICEF (2021a) through the Children's Climate Risk Index (CCRI). The CCRI is based on a multi-layered analysis of children's vulnerabilities – at the individual, community, national, and institutional levels – to the impacts of shocks and stresses, combined with the hazards of experiencing multiple, overlapping climate and environmental risks.[4]

---

[4] The risk index calculation is based on two factors: (1) children's exposure to climate and environmental shocks and stresses (e.g., water scarcity, floods, cyclones, heatwaves, air pollution) and (2) children's vulnerability (e.g., health and nutrition, education, poverty, communication, and social protection).

The risks of children's exposure to the impacts of climate change for 163 countries are calculated, ranging from 8.7 for children in the Central African Republic to 1.0 for children in Iceland. The index documents that almost all countries in Africa and Asia have very high CCRI scores, almost every child is exposed to at least one serious climate and environmental hazard, and 850 million children – approximately one-third of all children globally – are exposed to four or more stresses, leading to the conclusion that the climate crisis 'is already having a devastating impact on the well-being of children globally' (UNICEF, 2021a, p. 9).

Children are the most vulnerable to climate change because of their level of physical and cognitive development (e.g., immature neural and immune systems, less capacity to detect danger) and due to common age-specific behaviours (American Public Health Association (APHA), 2019; UNICEF, 2021a). Compared to adults, children breathe more air and drink more fluid for their body weight, and they are shorter, spend more time on the ground, and engage in more hand-to-mouth activities (APHA, 2019). All these factors increase their vulnerability to air, water, and soil pollutant exposures and disease vectors. Older children engage in more outdoor activities, resulting in greater exposure to heat and outdoor air pollution, which is exacerbated by climate change (APHA, 2019). Children are also vulnerable because of their dependency on adults. As discussed in subsection 2.2, in disaster situations, parents and other carers are likely to be stressed and preoccupied, and at worst, unavailable (e.g., through death, injury, separation), resulting in suboptimal care and protection of children. Furthermore, as discussed in Section 1, today's children are likely to experience multiple climate-related stressors whose impacts will accumulate over their lives.

Here we provide an overview of the known impacts on children's well-being of exposure to slower-onset changes caused by climate change, more sudden-onset events, and the more general environmental degradation and stresses that both cause. It is important to note that the literature tends to focus more on the impacts of sudden climate-related disasters than slower climate events like sea-level rise and increasing temperatures. Furthermore, the existing literature on disasters has paid more attention to physical health impacts than to psychosocial consequences.

Because climate change is an overarching factor in the macrosystem of children's lives, over time its impacts filter through other systems, including children's individual health, their interpersonal relationships, and the living conditions in their communities (Sanson, Wachs, et al., 2018; Sanson et al., 2022). Using the bioecological model (Figure 1), we present impacts at the individual level, including the physical and psychosocial impacts on

children. Then we discuss the available literature on the impacts at the micro-
and mesosystem levels, that is, impacts on the settings closest to children
such as family and neighbourhood. Then we explore the impacts at societal
and institutional levels. This framework helps to emphasise that no child
lives in a silo, but that the dynamics occurring within their families and
societies can exacerbate or ameliorate the extent to which children are
impacted by climate change.

2.1 Individual Impacts

Climate change exacerbates existing health threats and creates new ones.
Individual impacts not only affect children's current health conditions, but the
harm can last for many years resulting in a lifetime of lost opportunity
(UNICEF, 2021a) and even be passed down from generation to generation.
Climate change disrupts basic amenities, creating water crises, food insecurity,
biodiversity loss, and increasing levels of pollution in the air and soil. Climate
change therefore has myriad physical health impacts including respiratory
infections and illnesses, malnutrition, and vector- and water-borne infectious
diseases (Fuller et al., 2021; Milman, 2021).

The prevalence of vector-borne diseases, such as malaria, dengue, Lyme
disease, and Zika, is likely to increase with increasing temperatures and changing
climatic conditions that lead to the proliferation of mosquitoes and other vectors
(Blakstad & Smith, 2020). Over one in four children globally (600 million
children) are currently exposed to vector-borne diseases (UNICEF, 2021a),
which have potentially lasting health impacts such as neurological damage,
malnutrition, and developmental impairment (Anderko et al., 2020; Blakstad &
Smith, 2020). Zika, in particular, has adverse effects on children's physical,
cognitive, and mental well-being, intensifying social and economic inequalities
(Blakstad & Smith, 2020). Salinity from seawater intrusion is another conse-
quence of climate change that potentially creates public health hazards through its
impacts on freshwater availability for households, commercial use, agriculture,
and coastal ecosystems. For example, recent literature has shown that high salt
intake related to increasing water salinity increases the risks of miscarriage and
pre-eclampsia in pregnant women (Hossain, 2020).

Prenatal and early years exposure to climate shocks undermines children's
health by causing low birth weight and short height for age (Anderko et al.,
2020; Molina & Saldarriaga, 2017; Pacheco, 2020). For example, Kumar and
colleagues (2016) found that in utero exposure to droughts in India had detrimental impacts on children's nutritional status, with the impacts on child health
being mediated through financial duress in drought years.

Turning from slower-acting climate effects to more immediate ones, exposure to climate shocks and disasters that are increasing in frequency and ferocity (e.g., hurricanes, cyclones, wildfires, heatwaves, and floods) can have devastating physical impacts on children, ranging from illnesses to injuries and even death. Children are more likely than adults to suffer injuries and other physical afflictions during disasters (Biswas et al., 2010), which can lead to increased incidence of permanent disabilities, and disasters also disproportionately affect children with pre-existing disabilities (Stough et al., 2017). Disruptions to the basic necessities of life such as clean water, adequate food, and shelter result in health problems including respiratory conditions, stomach diseases, and malnutrition (Naylor, 2021; Peek et al., 2018).

The devastating shocks and continuous threats caused by climate change damage not only children's physical well-being but also their mental health. High levels of post-traumatic stress disorder (PTSD) have been reported in various humanitarian settings worldwide, with long-term effects on the lives of children (Kulig & Dabravolskaj, 2020; Leppold et al., 2022). For example, after the 2010 floods in Pakistan, 73 per cent of children aged ten to nineteen years displayed high levels of PTSD, with displaced girls more affected (Gibbons, 2014). Research analysing the psychosocial impacts of wildfires on children and their families showed that younger children who experienced significant exposure to the fire were more likely to experience PTSD than older children (Kulig et al., 2018; Kulig & Dabravolskaj, 2020). As another example, a study of 159 students aged eight to eighteen years after the 2005 bushfires in Australia found that, while most students reported having mild PTSD symptoms, substantial proportions reported moderate (17 per cent) or severe/very severe (10 per cent) symptoms, with younger children reporting more severe symptoms than older youth (Yelland et al., 2010).

The literature also documents the high risk of developing other mental health problems including depression, anxiety, substance abuse, phobias, sleep disorders, attachment disorders, regressive behaviours, and somatic complaints as a result of exposure to climate-related disasters (Anderko et al., 2020; Burke, et al., 2018). For children who experience multiple climate-related disasters, there can be cumulative mental health impacts, especially if they do not receive adequate support (Leppold et al., 2022; Sanson, Burke & Van Hoorn, 2018).

Most of the literature on the impacts of climate change on children's mental health focuses on climate-related disasters, but some literature provides evidence of links between slower environmental changes and poorer mental health (Burke et al., 2018; Clayton, 2020). For example, researchers in Canada and South Korea found associations between exposure to air pollution (known to be exacerbated by climate change) and symptoms of depression and suicide attempts (Trombley et al., 2017). Psychological impacts can also contribute to other developmental complications like problems with emotion regulation, behavioural issues, impaired language development, and impaired learning (Anderko et al., 2020; Burke et al., 2018).

2.2 Interpersonal Impacts

When looking at interpersonal impacts, climate stressors impact the physical and mental health of caregivers, thereby limiting their capacity to provide care and protection for children. For example, Biswas and colleagues (2010) found a high prevalence of unintentional injuries to children after floods in Bangladesh. They explained that, when caregivers were preoccupied with post-flood cleaning and reconstruction activities, children spent more time without adult supervision which increased the risks for them. Another study in Puerto Rico exploring the impacts on women and their children after Hurricane Maria showed that higher stress and depression scores among mothers were associated with higher negative affect and lower self-regulation in infants (Martinez, 2020). An increase of domestic violence after Hurricane Katrina in the USA was also reported by participants in a study by Harville et al. (2011).

Pressures on caregivers arise not only because of exposure to extreme weather events but also due to gradually unfolding environmental changes combined with existing economic and social challenges, resulting in anxiety about future loss and the well-being of future generations. A study conducted in Tuvalu found that the impacts of climate change (e.g., drought, more variable weather, and extreme temperatures) were predominant matters of concern in the community and that such concerns had increased since Tropical Cyclone Pam in 2015 (Gibson et al., 2019). A fifty-year-old participant said: 'I worry about my grandchildren, my children. I always tell them, "if something happens, or before the thing happens, you should migrate. Go to some place higher than Tuvalu"' (p. 679).

Environmental shocks produced by climate change increase household vulnerability, resulting in economic hardship, food and water insecurity, and, with extreme events, uninhabitable living conditions. The actions that families may take to try to face challenging circumstances can create harmful situations for children such as migration (Earle, 2021; Kielland & Kebede, 2020), child labour, and child marriage (Dewi & Dartanto, 2019; Guarcello et al., 2010). These practices affect adolescents more than children, but even young children become involved in child labour to support their families, which places them at higher risk of suffering violence and other threats as well as disrupting their education. Pereznieto and colleagues (2020) found that child labour usually occurs in industries that contribute to global carbon emissions and expose children to harmful chemicals like pesticides that have health and psychological consequences. Furthermore, the disruptions resulting from extreme weather events create and reinforce vulnerable conditions where child protection issues are more likely to occur. Research highlights the increased risk for children of experiencing different types of violence, including neglect, corporal punishment, sexual abuse, sex trafficking, and gender-based violence in the context of such events (Alston et al., 2014; Biswas et al., 2010; Rubenstein & Stark, 2017).

Evidence from Indigenous communities indicates that the changing climate can lead to changes in traditions and practices related to caring for children. For example, in Masai communities changing climate makes it difficult to maintain the custom for women to take a few months off from community labour to focus on care of their newborn babies, recover from giving birth, and receive special foods (like meat and milk) to ensure adequate nutrition (Leleto & Rehse, 2021).

The impacts on education are also well documented in the literature. Climate disasters often lead to children dropping out of school or reducing their school attendance, damage to school infrastructure, and school buildings becoming unavailable when used as shelters for displaced people (Harris & Hawrylyshyn, 2012; Krishna, Ronan & Alisic, 2018). Even if there is no interruption in school attendance, distress and disruption can impact children's mental health which, in turn, affects their academic performance (Gibbs et al., 2019; Scott et al., 2014). Furthermore, the impacts on physical health discussed earlier can prevent children from attending schools regularly.

Climate change can contribute to and exacerbate other humanitarian crises such as armed conflicts. It can create social instability and reduce community cohesion. More and more conflicts relate to tensions over access to land and natural resources that are becoming more precarious due to climate change (Akresh, 2016; Devonald et al., 2020). The adverse impacts of conflicts include the risk of physical injury or death, food and water insecurity, mental health impacts, and forced migration. A study on the effects of drought on Ethiopian adolescents found that many were forced to flee intense and widespread violence due to tensions over land use and grazing rights (Devonald et al., 2020). Forced migration poses multiple risks for children, both when moving from one place to another, and later when facing continuous challenges in the new destination (Maternowska et al., 2018).

As noted previously, climate change increases the spread of vector-borne diseases, increasing the risks for epidemics and pandemics. A current example is the COVID-19 pandemic whose impacts have gone far beyond physical health to include increased mental health difficulties (Marazziti et al., 2021), family stress, disruptions to education, and heightened economic pressures on families, undermining families' ability to meet children's care and emotional needs (Bornstein, 2021; Padilla & Bernheim, 2020).

2.3 Community and Societal Impacts

Climate change is reinforcing existing social and economic vulnerabilities as well as historical inequalities and disparities which is particularly important for children living in the Global South. Children in this region are already experiencing the disproportionate burden of adverse environmental and geopolitical impacts of climate change (Swaminathan et al., 2014), reflected in their high rankings on UNICEF's (2021a) CCRI. Vulnerable groups face even higher risks associated with climate change. The research identifies the following populations as especially vulnerable: girls, Indigenous children, Afro-descendant children, children living in poverty, children with chronic health conditions, and children with developmental disabilities (Fuller et al., 2021; Krishna, Majeed, et al., 2018; Leleto & Rehse, 2021; Stough et al., 2017).

For instance, child labour that is practised by families to cope with economic hardship caused by climate shocks is more common in countries with lower economic development such as those in Sub-Saharan Africa which are also experiencing severe climate shocks. It is estimated that 23.9 per cent of children and adolescents aged five to seventeen years in this region are involved in child labour (ILO & UNICEF, 2021). Boys are more likely than girls to be engaged in paid work outside the home (Putnick & Bornstein, 2016). As discussed earlier, child labour is associated with a myriad of risks for children, including child protection, education, and health issues. Hence, climate change is contributing to the perpetuation and exacerbation of social and economic disparities and prevents children from reaching their full potential.

2.4 Concluding Section Comments

In summary, despite insufficient research to date, it is clear that climate change acts in multiple ways to undermine children's health, well-being, and development. Sudden climate-driven disasters and slower-acting climate changes can have direct effects on individual children, and at least equally significant are effects occurring through impacts on their families, communities, and societies (Sanson et al., 2022). Whatever the mechanism, children who are already disadvantaged, whether due to their individual characteristics such as gender and disabilities, their families' socio-economic position, or geographic conditions, are those who suffer most. Overall, therefore, the conclusion by UNICEF's Executive Director Henrietta Fore (UNICEF, 2021b, para 16) that climate change is 'creating incredibly challenging environments for children to live, play and thrive' appears to be well founded.

3 Children's Knowledge and Feelings about Climate Change

This section builds on the review in Section 2 of the direct and indirect effects of varied climate change shocks on children's health and well-being by focusing on children's knowledge of and feelings about climate change.

3.1 How Children in the Global South Think and Feel about Climate Change

Children living in the Global South face the greatest climate risks, including their own death and the death of loved ones, physical injuries, PTSD and other psychological disturbances, social isolation, and forced migration. However, there is a dearth of systematic research on levels of climate knowledge and concerns for children and youth in this region. For example, when Lee and colleagues (2020) reviewed fifty-one studies of youth's perceptions of climate change, they found only five carried out in Asia, one in Latin America, and none in Africa. From the evidence available, they concluded that belief and concern about climate change are closely aligned and generally higher in lower-middle and upper-middle income countries than in the high-income countries in the Global North.

Most of what we know about children in the Global South comes from UN agencies and NGOs that carry out projects to mitigate impacts of climate change with children, youth, and families living in high-risk, low-income countries. These reports show that children frequently demonstrate informal knowledge and express concern about the risks facing themselves, their families, and communities. In general, reports focus on how disaster risk reduction and disaster response projects increase children's knowledge and promote their sense of agency and active responses, rather than discussing children's emotional responses. However, photos in these reports clearly convey children's emotional responses, and some studies reviewed include children's quotes which describe emotional reactions including worry, fear, helplessness, despair, and concern. It is likely that for at least some children in these studies, the feelings aroused by their experience of climate risks have prompted their active participation in NGO projects to mitigate climate change (as discussed further in Sections 4 and 8). In the paragraphs below, we summarise evidence of children's awareness of climate change and emotional responses to it for various regions in the Global South.

Africa. Reports from UN agencies and NGOs and stories in the media provide information on African children's experiences, knowledge, and responses to climate change. Twenty-three of the twenty-five countries with the highest

CCRI scores are in Sub-Saharan Africa (UNICEF, 2021a). In this region, children and families have historically faced droughts, extreme heat, and floods, all of which are amplified by climate change. Goumandakoye and Munang (2014, pp. 72–73) emphasised that children throughout Africa know that climate change is real and makes their lives and the lives of their families much harder:

> The effects of longer and more intense droughts, repeated floods, and shifting seasons are severely hampering their education and creating community pressures that result in children being more at risk from economic exploitation . . . Breaks in the regular water supply, for example, are costing a family of six in rural Africa an average of three hours a day that now has to be spent on the collection of water. Given that this is an activity predominantly carried out by children, the long-distance search for water is depriving them of time that could be spent on other activities, including school attendance.

A report from Polack (2010, p. 18) conveyed the despair and hopelessness Kenyan village children feel when witnessing the impacts of long-term climate change on their parents and community: 'We used to see parents going to the farm – but now children just see them sitting and making charcoal' (quote from female primary school student, Mazola Village, Kenya).

Asia and the Pacific. This region is home to four billion people – 60 per cent of the world's population (UNICEF et al., 2020). More than half live in low-lying coastal zones and floodplains that are extremely vulnerable to climate change. Despite the large population and the region's vulnerability, there are few studies of Asian and Pacific Islander children's knowledge and feelings about climate change. For example, an Indian study found that 90 per cent of students aged eleven to sixteen years were 'very' or 'quite' worried about global warming, but most were older than twelve (Chhokar et al., 2011).

However, UN agencies and NGOs have carried out numerous projects in this region that investigate children's and adolescents' knowledge about climate change, educate them further, and support their efforts to adapt to and mitigate the risks of climate change. Their reports document high levels of worry and concern throughout the region (e.g., Rello & Ackers, 2020). For example, a major research project conducted by international NGOs in partnership with local communities (UNICEF et al., 2020) assessed knowledge of climate change and disaster risks among 8,268 children and youth from twelve Asian and Pacific Island countries. More than 99 per cent reported having experienced one or more climate-related disasters within the past year. When asked to rank 14 possible concerns about their future, participants aged ten to fifteen years ranked the climate crisis as their top concern. Min Kant Naing, eleven years, from Myanmar, wrote this description about his experiences and active involvement in a children's group:

> There have some disasters in our community. Most common are severe heat waves, hail, heavy rain, and tropical storms. During the heavy rains there're usually floods. We have to use boats to go to schools. The name of our group is "Superhero children" because we want to be examples and hero to our community. If the climate worsens, not just trees, but also people will die. Because we are connected. Trees can provide oxygen and if trees are gone, people will die eventually. (UNICEF et al., 2020, p. 10).

Based on their personal experiences and knowledge, many of these young people wished to take action and discussed plans for contacting government officials to propose ideas for how to better address disaster risk and reduction.

We turn from this multinational study to a study of communities in one city in the Philippines. Berse's (2017) research with Filipino children and adolescents adopted a bioecological approach so we discuss it in some detail. It addressed participants' experiences, knowledge, feelings, and coping responses to climate changes and, importantly, described the protections and support available from children's families (microsystem), from city and community (mesosystem), and from the national government (macrosystem).

Berse collected information from forty-five children and adolescents aged nine to fifteen living in three neighbouring communities in Malolos, a city north of Manila, to understand how they perceived and responded to the impacts of climate change. These communities are increasingly exposed to impacts of climate change, and the children and adolescents received differing levels of support depending on family and community resources. Pamarawan is an island with a small community of families who have lived there for generations; Longos is a community with many employed and stable families; Bangkal has more poor families who are recent arrivals.

Berse found that children's and adolescents' knowledge about climate change was primarily acquired informally through their direct experiences. They related climate change to frequent extreme weather events, such as flooding following typhoons. Some knew that climate change led to the slower changes they experienced such as increased heat and rising sea levels. Some had learned about climate change through mass media and in school but, without mandated curriculum, what was taught depended on teachers' interest and knowledge.

The children described their experience and knowledge of extreme heat, heavy rains, cyclones and flooding, their feelings, and the actions they took.

Storms and floods often made work and school impossible. Children found cyclones terrifying and described 'the sight of roofs being blown away, trees being uprooted, and "tidal waves surging inland"' (p. 222). Extreme weather events leading to evacuations posed further difficulties: '[Children] reported mixed feelings from being scared to sad to having a difficult time adjusting to the rationed food, limited space, and generally chaotic environment in many temporary shelters' (p. 223). As Berse explained, 'some children, especially those who are from poor families, reported feelings of helplessness and exasperation in performing individual level interventions without corresponding long-term action from the community' (p. 223).

Berse emphasised that poorer children knew they faced greater risks than those whose families could afford to protect them more. A nine-year-old boy from Longos shared his distress: 'We don't get to eat because our parents could not get to work' (p. 222). Poor children from Pamarawan were exceptions worth noting because families on this island had lived together for generations and helped each other in times of adversity. Overall, the children received little or no support from the city or national government, with Berse noting that no government measures explicitly paid attention to the needs of children.

Latin America. Climate change impacts in Latin America (comprising South America, Central America, the Caribbean, and Mexico) include droughts, extreme heat, floods, and hurricanes. Across the entire region, nine out of ten children are exposed to at least two overlapping environmental and climate change shocks (UNICEF, 2021a). With few research studies available, UN agencies and NGOs provide the most information about children's knowledge and feelings related to climate change in this region. For example, a 2021 UNICEF newsletter entitled 'Normal life washed away in Guatemala' described the disastrous impact of Hurricanes Eta and Iota that led to landslides and massive flooding across the region (UNICEF, 2021c). More than 900,000 children in Guatemala were affected, including nine-year-old Juana from Campur, a town previously landlocked and surrounded by lush forest but now under water after the flood. Juana recounted her experience:

> "My dad used to sell things at the farm supplies store over there," Juana, 9, says as she points over the water from a boat, navigating the remains of her hometown. "This was a mill. There used to be a store over there. . . . I think that was our kitchen. Here was the church. There's the gate. It makes me sad to see it. . . . I try not to remember because it just makes me sad . . . What if we had died under water? It was best to go . . . " (para 1).

3.2 How Children in the Global North Think and Feel about Climate Change

Even a few years ago, many children and families in the Global North thought that climate change was real but happening to others far away. The rising numbers of extreme weather events as well as droughts and other slower impacts of climate change have literally brought home the reality of the climate crisis to many in the Global North. Also significant have been young people's leadership and participation in global demonstrations to call citizens and governments to action. From a bioecological perspective, it is therefore likely that children in the Global North will show increasing levels of knowledge and concern over time.

Australia and New Zealand are among the wealthy, educated, and industrialised countries in the Asia-Pacific region. In contrast to poorer countries in the region, they have low Climate Change Risk Indices of 3.6 and 1.6, respectively. But here, too, knowledge and concern have grown as the threats of climate change become more widespread and more personally relevant, with many people witnessing warming land and sea temperatures and, especially in Australia, unprecedented bushfires, floods, and droughts.

The importance of place and personal experience is underscored by research before and after wildfires (e.g., Harker-Schuch et al., 2021; Kulig & Dabravolskaj, 2020). Towers and colleagues (2020) investigated Australian children's knowledge of bushfire emergency responses, conducting focus groups with eighty-seven children aged eight to twelve years who lived in four bushfire-prone locations in south-eastern Australia. These children knew about the danger of bushfires and the vital importance of preparing for future emergencies, such as decisions on what to take, where the family planned to meet or to shelter, and plans for where to live.

The importance of personal experience and place is also evident in McDonald-Harker et al.'s study (2022) of the responses of Canadian children and adolescents to the 2013 Alberta flood. The researchers interviewed eighty-three children and adolescents aged five to fifteen years after the flood and found significant changes in their views and environmental practices. For example, Javier, a seven-year-old, talked about his feelings about the devastation: 'I was like thinking about the flood today cause, it made me sad... remembering about the trees and plants' (p. 14). Twelve-year-old Melissa explained: 'I definitely do [think more] because after the flood I realised that we're actually living here, and this can happen any time. Then I started to notice that there were a whole bunch of different kinds of issues with our world' (p.18). Many children thought of climate change as the root cause of the flood. Afterwards they were motivated to take action themselves and call others to action to ameliorate climate and environmental problems.

Lee and Barnett (2020) investigated the questions that UK children asked rather than their responses to questions adults ask them about climate change. This approach privileges children as active agents who engage in issues that interest them. Children aged twelve to fourteen years asked climate scientists their own questions in on-line chat sessions. Using thematic analysis, Lee and Barnett analysed the 820 questions related to climate change. They identified six categories: the nature of climate change, its causes, current impacts, future impacts (the largest category), solutions (second largest category), and the reality/severity of climate change. Lee and Barnett concluded that the students' questions showed they were well aware of the potential seriousness of many current and future impacts of climate change and understood the importance of implementing solutions.

3.3 Adolescents' and Young Adults' Emotional Reactions to the Climate Crisis

In contrast to the limited research on children's knowledge and emotional reactions related to climate change, there is a growing literature on adolescents' and young adults' climate change knowledge and concerns showing growing levels of knowledge along with strong emotions (e.g., Lee et al., 2020). A recent online survey of 10,000 youth aged sixteen to twenty-five years from the Global North and Global South led Hickman and her colleagues (Hickman et al., 2021) to conclude that children and young people from countries in all parts of the world are experiencing levels of climate anxiety and dissatisfaction with governmental responses high enough to impact their everyday functioning. Almost 60 per cent of respondents reported feeling 'very' or 'extremely' worried about climate change. Across all countries, 58 per cent of young people reported feelings of betrayal due to their government's inadequate responses to the climate crisis, and this sense of betrayal correlated with their level of climate anxiety. Furthermore, 58 per cent felt that humanity is actually doomed.

A survey conducted by the Pew Research Center (Bell et al., 2021) in wealthier countries in the Global North and Global South found that younger people were more concerned than adults about climate change. For example, 65 per cent of respondents aged eighteen to twenty-nine in Sweden indicated they were 'very/somewhat concerned' compared to 25 per cent of those aged sixty-five and over.

Other research on adolescents' and young adults' emotional responses reveals that strong emotions including the following are common: hopelessness, anger, anxiety, worry, grief, fear, vulnerability, numbness, and uncertainty about their future (e.g., Clayton, 2020; Coffey et al., 2021; Cunsolo et al., 2020; Dodds, 2021; Pihkala, 2020; Sanson et al., 2018). Because climate concerns are unlikely to start abruptly in adolescence, it is highly probable that younger children are also experiencing these sorts of emotional responses but the lack of large-scale surveys on this age group precludes firm conclusions. Clearly further research investigating children's emotional responses to climate change is critically needed.

Terms commonly used to describe these feelings include eco-anxiety, eco-distress, climate change anxiety, climate distress and climate anxiety, and the term 'solastalgia' describes the painful emotions that people have following the loss of loved places (Albrecht et al., 2007). Researchers have attempted to distinguish among these terms (e.g., Coffey et al., 2021), but the media typically uses the term 'eco-anxiety'. Clayton and colleagues (2017, p. 68) defined eco-anxiety as 'a chronic fear of environmental doom'. However, this term tends to imply a psychopathological disorder, whereas it can be regarded as a healthy, rational response to catastrophic dangers. Clayton (2020) noted that it is important to distinguish between anxiety that is maladaptive and adaptive. Although Wu and colleagues (2020) reported that anxiety about climate change can lead to obsessive thinking, insomnia, and/or panic attacks, it is rarely pathological (Hickman et al., 2021). In contrast, climate distress is adaptive when it alerts us to danger and motivates us to take effective actions. Or, as Lawton (2019, para.12) described it, 'We could say that the outbreak of "climate anxiety" is not an outbreak of mental illness, but represents a long overdue outbreak of sanity'.

3.4 Concluding Section Comments

The dearth of research on younger children's knowledge of and feelings about climate change has important implications for researchers and practitioners worldwide. Some potential reasons for this worldwide lack of research attention to children, particularly in the Global South, are explored in Section 8. It is clear, however, that the majority of adolescents do know and are worried. Knowledge and worries presumably do not simply emerge *de novo* but develop over time. Given the increasingly global impacts of climate change, widespread media coverage, and massive global protests, it is highly likely that many children – even young children – know and are worried about the climate crisis.

To best support children – especially in the midst of this global crisis – we need to understand how children's knowledge and emotional responses develop over time and in what contexts. Few studies exist that give a clear understanding of developmental and experiential processes involved, and few take a holistic perspective. This scarcity of research should be of serious concern to developmental scientists and must be remedied. To date, we know little about children's personal experiences and knowledge of the impacts of climate change over time; the actions they take to adapt to these impacts; their families' experiences and reactions; the support and resources that their family, community, and government provide; climate change education in their schools and communities; and information they receive from the media. Bioecological theory has practical implications for researchers and practitioners with its focus on systems from the individual to the macro-level. In addition to analyses of variables like country, age, gender, and socio-economic status, researchers could include data related to children's physical abilities and experiences, such as injury, disabilities, disease, death of loved ones, school disruptions, evacuations, and forced migration. Future research on children's feelings could investigate whether and to whom children from different backgrounds and cultures express their concerns, worries, and anxieties. Last, it is vital that future research and intervention programs actively contribute to the well-being of children in the Global South as well as Global North.

4 Coping with Climate Change

Section 3 has shown that many children know about climate change and are worried about its impacts. Here we examine how children are coping with climate change, what strategies they use, and how effective they are. This discussion builds our understanding of how best to help children to manage the climate crisis and all that it entails. Coping with the climate crisis is about managing the problem as well as the distressing feelings that it engenders. Coping, or adapting psychologically, includes how children make sense of climate change, how they manage the associated feelings, and how they engage with the problem and respond practically, socially, and politically.

4.1 Children's Use of Emotion-, Problem- and Meaning-Focused Coping Strategies for Dealing with Climate Change

Much of the early research looking at how children and young people cope with climate change was conducted by Ojala (2012a) who studied Swedish children from late childhood (average age eleven) through to early adulthood to learn how they were coping with emotions evoked by the complex challenges of climate change, and whether different ways of handling negative feelings could hinder or promote learning, competence, mental health, and well-being. Ojala's research built on the work by Folkman and Lazarus (Folkman, 2008; Lazarus & Folkman, 1984) on emotion-focused, problem-focused, and meaning-focused coping as three distinct ways in which people cope with adversity and challenges.

Emotion-focused coping refers to the ways in which children try to regulate or eliminate uncomfortable feelings about the climate crisis. Ojala (2012b) found that some children and young people used techniques like distraction, avoidance, and deliberately thinking about other things. For example, a child in the intermediate school-age group (average age eleven) using distraction said: 'I usually sing because when I do I really calm down, and then I try to think about something else' (Ojala, 2012b, p. 545). A smaller number (usually those showing low levels of climate concern) minimised or de-emphasised the severity of climate change, framing it as a problem that they themselves do not have to worry about (e.g., 'I would say there's no danger of any floods as long as we're alive' – intermediate school pupil, p. 545), or even denying the problem of climate change. The most commonly used technique for all age groups (but particularly for younger children) was distancing from the worry (e.g., 'I think about something fun', p. 545). Children also used social support – talking to family or friends about their concerns – to regulate uncomfortable feelings.

Emotion-focused coping was associated not only with higher levels of subjective well-being than problem-focused coping (next section), but also with lower levels of environmental action, and served more to regulate worry than to promote hope for the future. That is, emotion-focused strategies helped the children to feel better but they did not increase children's involvement in doing something about the problem and were thus less constructive ways of coping, at least in terms of engaging in action on climate change (Ojala, 2021).

Problem-focused coping strategies refer to children's efforts to solve the problem which is causing the stress. In Ojala's research, children undertook both individual and collective pro-environmental actions and adopted these strategies almost as commonly as emotion-focused strategies to try to regulate worry (except for younger children who used distancing more than action). Individual behaviours included preparing for action (e.g., learning about the problem, planning what to do), and environmentally friendly actions, like bicycling to school, recycling, conserving household energy, and encouraging others to act. The collective problem-focused coping strategies included considering ways in which problems can be solved more easily if people work together.

Children who used problem-focused coping had higher environmental efficacy beliefs as measured with items such as 'I/we together can do something about climate change'. They were more likely to take action to protect the environment, but many of these children also expressed lower subjective well-being (Ojala, 2012a, 2013). In this and later research, Ojala and other researchers (Ojala, 2016a; Stevenson & Peterson, 2016) found that young people almost always reported individual household actions when describing their problem-focused coping strategies (e.g., recycling) rather than collective activities. Ojala (2016a) argued that this trend could account for the relation between problem-focused coping and lower well-being because research has found that, when a problem is more than one person can solve alone, individual strategies can lead to feelings of futility and reduce well-being (Clarke, 2006). Berse's (2017) study (discussed in Section 3) of climate impacts and coping in nine- to fifteen-year-old Filipino children also illustrated this. Most children used problem-focused rather than emotion-focused coping strategies (e.g., waste management, tree planting, cleaning flood-prone areas), but some reported helplessness and exasperation in performing individual-level interventions without corresponding long-term action from the community.

The third type of coping identified by Ojala is meaning-focused coping (Ojala, 2016a) where children used different ways of thinking about the problem of climate change to regulate their worry and promote hope. One meaning-focused technique was positive reappraisal – reframing the situation to see its positive sides, like taking an historical perspective, noting how much more attention is now being paid to the problem than previously; or recognising that other seemingly insurmountable problems (e.g., apartheid, slavery) have been solved in the past through the sustained actions of committed people. Another meaning-focused technique was to deliberately cultivate positive thinking to promote hope. Children described trying to focus on the positive aspects and believe that the problem will be solved in the future because, as one of the younger children said, 'No hope, no reason to live' (Ojala, 2012b, p. 547).

A third meaning-focused technique was to cultivate trust in different societal actors like scientists, environmental organisations, businesses, politicians, and citizens working for climate solutions, and build hope from recognising that millions of people worldwide share the same concerns and are developing new ways to address climate change. This thinking helps young people to feel less alone with their concerns. Berse also noted 'trust in fate, if not faith in God' (Berse, 2017, p. 223) as an additional coping strategy among his Filipino participants.

Children of all ages in Ojala's research reported using meaning-focused coping strategies, although less commonly than emotion- and problem-focused coping. They used these strategies more to promote hope than to regulate worry. Younger children were more likely to use meaning-focused coping than older children, and their most commonly used technique was trust – and particularly trust in scientists. 'I think somebody is going to invent something good for nature and all the people and animals' (Ojala, 2012b, p. 548).

Importantly, meaning-focused coping was related to several positive outcomes. Ojala (2015) reported that young people who used meaning-focused coping techniques also reported greater well-being and life satisfaction, a higher sense of purpose and optimism, and more active engagement in environmental issues, despite serious climate concerns.

As discussed in Sections 2 and 3, children are suffering both physically and psychologically as a result of the climate crisis, so understanding how they cope is vitally important. Whilst Ojala's research has focused mainly on children and young people in Sweden (a wealthy country currently relatively buffered from negative climate impacts), it nevertheless established a very helpful framework for understanding some of the different strategies that children use to cope.

In the next section we examine other research on how children in other parts of the world cope with and respond to climate change. Some of these strategies fit neatly into Ojala's framework. Others do not but are nonetheless important strategies for children to use to respond to the threat of climate change.

4.2 Regulating Emotions through Social Support, Talking about Feelings, and Time in Nature

Talking with trusted others and sharing and expressing difficult feelings have long been recognised as key to helping children (and adults) to regulate their feelings (e.g., Breuer & Freud, 1895/2001; Gottman & Declaire, 1998), and a body of research examines the use of these strategies in coping with adversities like disasters (e.g., Pfefferbaum et al., 2014; see also Section 5). A related literature looks at the positive relation between social support and well-being in children exposed to disasters like extreme weather events (e.g., Gibbs et al., 2015; Lai et al., 2018).

Chawla (2020) reviewed research and reflections from educators and activists on how children cope with difficult emotions about the environment and how they conceive hope, and she summarised their findings in a converging list of practices. A key factor was young people being able to share their feelings and thoughts without judgement, as expressed thus: 'It is also important for young people to talk (and rant) about our feelings and experiences with people who support us, like parents, family, friends, and mentors who understand the issues. Humour can also help us diffuse our emotions' (Godden et al., 2021, p. 1762).

Engaging with nature often appears in the literature on how children cope with climate change but usually in the context of the mental health and psychologically restorative benefits of nature for children or its link with conservation behaviours (e.g., Chawla, 2020; see also Section 5), rather than as a deliberate coping strategy for climate distress. However, in a study of older (fifteen- to twenty-five-year-old) Inuit children from Labrador, MacDonald et al. (2015) reported that young people found solace for climate worries through getting out on the land and connecting with cultural practices such as fishing. More research is needed in this area to better understand the extent to which children actively seek out nature as a way of coping with their climate distress, and how effective this is as a strategy, especially when children are growing in their awareness of the damage being done to the very natural environment to which they are connecting.

4.3 Cultivating Hope as a Coping Strategy

Hope appears often in the coping literature. Ojala regards the promotion of hope as a meaning-focused coping strategy. She calls it constructive hope when children and young people are able to face environmental risks and uncertainty, believe that their own actions and the actions of others can make a difference, and find positive meaning in action (Ojala, 2016b). Other researchers have related the cultivation of hope to emotion-focused strategies of sharing thoughts and feelings about climate change (as discussed earlier). Some researchers also argue that children using their imagination, and then getting involved in action, cultivates hope. For example, Trott (2019) showed that helping children to imagine preferable futures for their community, and then identifying realistic steps to move towards them, seemed to help children feel less helpless about the climate crisis. Macy and Johnstone (2012) also explored the benefits of visioning as a way of cultivating active hope and motivating action on the climate crisis. Their three steps of active hope are (1) taking a clear view of reality, (2) seeing the direction the person would like things to move in, and (3) taking concrete steps to change things. However, these steps have not been formally researched with children.

4.4 Child Sense of Agency and Collective Action as a Form of Coping with Climate Change

Children and young people have been using 'action as an antidote to anxiety and despair' (Sanson et al., 2019) and as a way of coping with environmental problems for much longer than researchers have been studying it. Here we examine different types of collective action that children engage in around the world in response to environmental problems as well as what we currently know about the relation between collective action as a coping strategy and children's well-being.

Collective action both requires and builds belief in group (or collective) efficacy; that is, the belief that by working together on shared activities people can create change. It also develops children's sense of agency (the capacity and ability to take action by one's own free choices) by showing children that they themselves can effect change as a part of a larger movement (Hart et al., 2014).

Much of what we know about how children deal with climate change in the Global South comes from intergovernmental organisations and NGO reports that focus on children's adaptation to direct climate change impacts and mitigation of threats of future impacts in their communities. For example, a project by World Vision International (Cuevas-Parra, 2020) involving interviews with 121 children from twelve countries showed that most saw themselves as active contributors to climate action, via their involvement in community-led initiatives in disaster risk management, landscape restoration, and emission- and pollution-reduction projects. Children attested that it was important for them to transform information into action and explore different forms of activism, and thought that they achieved the best outcomes by acting as a group rather than as isolated individuals. Whilst this study did not specifically report on children's well-being following collective action, it is clear that responding to the problems of climate change by getting involved in collective solutions was important. Similar reports cited in Section 6 further illustrate this association.

Based on a review of extensive work on child/youth participation largely in the Global South, Hart et al. (2014) argued that children should be involved in community governance (all the ways in which communities manage themselves, often via community organisations), especially in poor and marginalised communities that lack public services. Children even as young as three can be supported to begin learning to manage their activities cooperatively. They concluded: 'taking action through playing a meaningful role in the face of adversity can offer psychological protection by helping children to feel more in control, more hopeful and more resilient' (p. 93).

In the Global North, much of the research on children engaging in collective action comes via formal and informal climate education programs (see Section 6 for examples). Researchers often report that participation helps children and young people gain environmental understanding and a sense of hope from working with others towards shared goals (e.g., Gallay et al., 2022). Again, we see the links between action on problems that impact children facing climate adversity, and the development of their hope, efficacy, and agency.

4.5 Collective Action in the Form of Activism: School Climate Strikes, Youth Mobilisation, and Youth-Led Litigation

When Greta Thunberg started striking from school outside the Swedish Parliament in August 2018 at age fifteen years, she sparked a massive wave of child-led activism[5] in the form of school strikes around the globe, and the following year an estimated four to six million people participated in more than 2,500 events in over 163 countries in the largest climate mobilisation in world history (Taylor et al., 2019). Young people had joined collective climate protests over previous decades, but the school strikes movement mobilised many more children, youth, families, and others across the world in vigorous campaigning to bring about sociopolitical action on the climate crisis.

Researchers are only beginning to examine the positive and negative outcomes for children and young people from participating in this sort of collective action or from joining a burgeoning number of youth-led organisations (e.g. Millennium Kids; School Strike 4 Climate). Sanson and Bellemo (2021) reported on interviews with older students who were engaged in school strikes or other activism. These young people explained how their activism helped them manage their anxiety about the future and channel it into determination, courage, and optimism. These students learned essential skills and capacities in collaborative problem-solving, community organising, non-violent communication, and public speaking, and they reported that participation could be highly rewarding and engaging. To sustain their mental health and engagement, young people cited the vital importance of having strong communities and support networks that hold space for their feelings.

However, youth activism can also create challenges. Some young respondents in Sanson and Bellemo's (2021) study reported feeling immense pressure, feeling that all the responsibility to protect the future was being put on their shoulders, and risked burnout, mental strain, and feeling overwhelmed. Other young people have reported that they did not have the opportunity to participate in collective action because they were 'not supported by their families or adults, or have caring responsibilities, and for many, particularly Aboriginal youth and young people of colour, the costs of 'getting into trouble' or missing school are too high' (Godden et al., 2021, p. 1761). Van Nieuwenhuizen et al. (2021) also reported that, although climate activism is associated with resilience and positive development, it may also be a source of increased stress, particularly for marginalised youth.

---

[5] The term 'activism', according to the Cambridge Dictionary, is 'the use of direct and noticeable action to achieve a result, usually a political or social one'.

Another increasingly common form of child-led action is litigation, where children and youth use legal courts to try to compel governments to take action on the climate crisis. Among a number of cases, in Colombia a child-led court action resulted in the Government being required to protect children's future environment and protect the Amazon rainforest in its own right (Our Children's Trust, 2018). In the USA, young people have brought a number of legal actions against governmental bodies demanding that they protect the environment, the lives of young people, and future generations (Our Children's Trust). In Australia in 2021, five fourteen- to twenty-five-year-olds from diverse backgrounds (including First Nations youth, youth with disabilities, and youth from communities which are facing acute climate change risks) lodged a number of human rights complaints with the United Nations over the Australian Government's failure to act to meaningfully cut greenhouse gas emissions by 2030 (Landis-Hanley, 2021).

In conclusion, the emerging body of research on collective action shows how it incorporates both problem-focused coping (undertaking action on the problem), emotion-focused coping (e.g., comfort and support from working with others), and meaning-focused coping (e.g., feeling hope through recognising others are working on the problem, and increased sense of efficacy in achieving change). This work has predominantly been conducted with older children and adolescents, but children of even preschool age participate in school strikes and other collective action, and it is likely that they also accrue benefits from their participation. Nonetheless, more research in this area is needed. For example, we do not know the extent to which being involved in such action actually *reduces* children's climate distress.

4.6 Concluding Section Comments

The important question for adults who care about children is no longer whether children worry about climate change (because they do), but what are the ways in which children cope with the climate crisis and how can adults support children to use effective ways of coping – not just with their distressing feelings, but also to promote their engagement with caring for and protecting the world. The limited available research reviewed in this section documents the variety of coping strategies that children use. Some strategies distance or distract children from the problem, and may be useful for avoiding distressing feelings, but do not help children feel more in control or hopeful, nor help children engage with the problem. More active coping strategies involve doing something about the problem, through learning about it, recognising that children are not alone in worrying about and acting on the climate crisis, and taking action themselves.

These strategies involve more pro-environmental actions and tend to build more efficacy and hope, but they can also have a range of emotional impacts.

As noted, the literature in this area is very sparse, most has focused on older children and adolescents, and very little has been conducted in the Global South. Little or no research has taken a fully developmental and culturally appropriate approach, examining processes underlying the development of different strategies in different contexts or how they develop over time. There is an urgent need for more research on all these issues which would help address how parents and educational programs can best support children to cope; these issues are the foci of the next two sections.

5 Parenting in the Age of Climate Crisis

Earlier sections of this Element have documented how climate change affects children differently around the world. However *all* parents, wherever they are, are in the unprecedented situation of having a responsibility to protect and prepare their children for an uncertain but definitely challenging climate-altered world. Following the review of children's different coping strategies in Section 4, here we discuss how parents[6] can best support children to cope with the climate crisis. The challenges for caregivers already facing significant environmental and socio-economic impacts differ from those for parents living where climate change is still largely a future threat, and we discuss both these contexts.

Little research looks directly at the efficacy of parental efforts to support their children around the overall threat of climate change, but a larger body of research exists on helping children cope with extreme climate-induced disasters. There is a growing collection of resources (e.g., tipsheets, articles) to guide parents, particularly in the Global North, on how to address children's questions, feelings, and responses to the climate crisis. These resources draw on expertise and research in psychology, disaster mental health, parenting, and education. In the following subsections we review common themes including guidance on talking with children about environmental threats, helping them cope with their feelings about climate change, and nurturing pro-environmental values, along with the evidence to support these strategies.

5.1 Helping Children Cope with Direct Impacts of Climate Change

What parents do to help children cope with direct climate change impacts, mainly extreme weather events, prior to, during, and after the event, is

---

[6] Here we use the term 'parent' to refer to any adult who is playing a caregiving role in a child's life, which could also include other relatives and community members, not just biological parents.

increasingly relevant to communities in both the Global South and Global North. Changes including hotter temperatures, more unstable weather, worsening fire seasons, and more dangerous extreme weather events mean that around the globe more families are affected by climate-related disasters, including being temporarily or permanently displaced from their communities.

Parents have a vital role in helping children cope with disasters. Before a disaster, they can involve children in emergency preparedness. They can also protect their children from direct exposure to risk during and after the event. For example, during extreme heat, they can keep children indoors or take them to cool public places to shelter.

Throughout and in the aftermath of a disaster, parents can call on a range of strategies to help children manage their anxieties: encouraging them to notice and name uncomfortable feelings (e.g., fear), to identify bodily cues that they are feeling anxious (e.g., sweating or shivering), to use relaxation techniques (e.g., progressive muscle relaxation exercises), to manage anxious self-talk, and to get involved in useful action (e.g., helping with recovery efforts). Parents are also encouraged to model their own effective coping skills (even if distressed), seek social support, and re-establish children's routines as quickly as possible (Ronan & Johnston, 2005). These strategies are also relevant for parents helping children who are displaced due to climate change, in addition to reconnecting children with education where possible, accessing healthcare, and protecting them from violence, although the larger systems in which parents are embedded can limit the extent to which parents can act, and how they can do so (Gaziulusoy, 2020).

In addition, disaster research emphasises the importance of cultivating hope (Hobfoll et al., 2007), helping children to see that their world is basically a safe place, people are usually good, and that life is worth living. Parents can help children to see some positive changes that come from distressing or tragic events, for example, noticing increased community kindness and helpfulness in the aftermath of disaster, having increased appreciation for relationships and loved ones, and finding positive things to do for others, so that children feel they can make a positive difference in the world (APS, 2016).

We know that children's capacity to cope in disasters rests in large part on their parents' coping and support (Ronan & Johnston, 2005), but there is actually very little research into parenting interventions designed to build parents' skills to help children cope. And even though 85 per cent of the world's children live in the Global South (in places most susceptible to climate change impacts), most of the literature on parents' roles in helping children adapt to disasters comes from the Global North. We have little systematic understanding of the roles that parents in the Global South play in actively helping their children prepare for and cope with direct climate impacts like extreme weather events. More research is needed here.

5.2 Helping Children Cope with the Indirect Impacts of Climate Change

5.2.1 Talking with Very Young Children about Climate Change

Young children think in concrete ways and are preoccupied with their immediate surroundings and familiar events and objects. They learn not just via what people tell them but by interacting with their world (Harris, 2012). Most advice for caregivers of young children (zero to six years) focuses on allowing children to 'fall in love with nature' or to 'hear the music of nature' around them (FOSS, 2017), rather than direct conversations about the climate crisis. Children first need time in nature, to feel comfortable in and as a part of nature, which leads to motivation to care for nature (Giusti et al., 2018; see Section 5.5 for more discussion).

However, it is important not to underestimate very young children's knowledge, curiosity, and competencies about environmental issues. Research by Engdahl (2015) in early childhood settings showed how even very young children think about their environment and act beyond their own self-interests. Advice to parents, drawing from this research, is that conversations with younger children can include noticing the seasons, caring for animals, planting seeds, learning concepts about sharing Earth's space with other living things, and cleaning up after ourselves to protect plants and animals' homes. Parents can express appreciation for the care that children take for nature to build their pro-environmental identity and values, thus encouraging children to continue to behave in these positive ways (Shinn, 2019).

Parents also need to be responsive to children's questions. Young children formulate questions as early as twelve months, and at around two and a half years they start asking more advanced 'how' and 'why' questions to elicit explanations and reasons (Harris, 2012). Questions like 'Why are those people marching? Why is it so smoky? Why are the plants here all black?' can be openers for simple conversations about how the climate is changing and our need to protect the Earth.

Two climate scientists who are also parents provided useful examples of key messages for parents to communicate to young children to help them understand the problem of climate change and what can be done about it. They recommended that conversations include: (1) This is the best planet! (e.g., 'We have everything we need here. The ocean, atmosphere, and land are all connected'); (2) Our climate is warming and we know why (e.g., 'Naturally occurring carbon dioxide acts like a cozy blanket, keeping us at the right temperature. Too much carbon dioxide makes it too hot'); (3) The bad news (e.g., 'The planet is more than two degrees hotter than it was before humans started putting carbon dioxide in the atmosphere. It's too many blankets. This doesn't sound like much, but if you were a few degrees hotter you'd have a fever!'); and (4) The good news (e.g., 'We have solutions! There are ways to get where we need to go, have things we need, and keep ourselves comfortable without changing the climate – peel off those blankets. We can't solve it unless we work together. But we can, and we will!') (C. Benitez-Nelson and K. Marvel, personal communication, 21 February 2022).

Finally, parents can model pro-environmental behaviours and provide simple explanations for their reasons for taking actions which set expectations for their young children to act similarly. For example, 'I don't use plastic shopping bags because they are made from coal and oil which are making the Earth too hot', or 'I catch the train to work because cars use petrol which makes the world too hot' (APS, 2018a).

5.2.2 Talking with School-Aged Children about Climate Change

Anecdotal reports and surveys show that parents often try to shield their children from the frightening truth of the climate crisis (e.g., Global Action Plan UK & Unilever, 2021), but this option is virtually impossible because of widespread media coverage (Sanson et al., 2018). The existing evidence suggests that the majority of older children know about climate change and worry about it, and anecdotal evidence suggests this is also true of younger children (see Section 3).

Environmental psychologist Clayton argues that trying to conceal the truth about the climate crisis can generate fear, harm a child's ability to trust, and skew children's objectivity about the climate crisis (Akpan, 2019). Furthermore, as outlined in the United Nations Convention on the Rights of the Child (UN, 1989), children have a right to learn about issues that affect their future, to have a voice and be involved in protecting themselves. Minimising the problem also risks invalidating children's deep concerns about the planet. According to Eklund and Nylén (2021), claiming that *silver bullet*[7] solutions will solve the problem can also be problematic because children who are aware of the scale of the climate crisis know that single technological solutions cannot be the whole answer and may feel even more helpless and hopeless when the adults around them seem to be relying on fantasies. However, finding a way to

---

[7] A common critique of ambitious mitigation scenarios is the over-reliance on a single mitigation strategy or technology, often referred to as a 'silver bullet'.

tell the truth about the climate crisis while also cultivating hope is one of the challenges parents face in supporting children to cope with climate change, and is discussed further later.

Through primary and secondary school, children develop more complex ways of thinking about the world and are expanding their horizons and interests. By late childhood, children are able to take a more global perspective, understand past/present/future connections and cause-and-effect relations. Conversations with older primary school-aged children can include simple explanations of the science of climate change, such as greenhouse gases and ocean acidification, using metaphors to help them understand, and increasing in complexity as children get older. Parents and children together researching answers to children's questions can be a supportive way for children to learn about climate change. By asking questions about children's knowledge about climate change, parents also have an opportunity to correct any misperceptions children might have about it (APS, 2017).

Listening to children and finding out what they are thinking and feeling about the climate crisis is critically important. In Hickman et al.'s (2021) study of 10,000 youth around the world, 48 per cent of those who had talked to others about climate change reported that they had been ignored or dismissed. For their child to feel supported and understood, parents need to listen carefully and validate their children's feelings of anxiety, fear, and anger as reasonable responses to the crisis, perhaps acknowledging that parents sometimes feel the same way (Sanson et al., 2018).

5.3 Supporting Children's Emotions and Cultivating Hope

As well as practical skills and knowledge, children need the right tools to cope with climate concerns. Reflections by researchers, environmental activists, and educators working on climate change produce converging lists of practices for helping children cope with difficult climate-related emotions and build hope, which are similar to those identified in earlier research on helping children cope with disasters, as well as the three types of coping strategies identified in the previous section.

Chawla (2020) summarised the key strategies: creating space to share emotions; listening to children's feelings; encouraging positive appraisal of the situation; encouraging children to take actions to address the problems (and envision futures they would like to see); and fostering social trust. If children and young people try to cope by expressing negative emotions, it is critical that parents, teachers, and others listening to them acknowledge, take seriously, and validate these expressed emotions (see APS, 2018b; Benoit et al., 2021). Parents also teach emotion regulation skills through modelling how they handle strong feelings themselves, recognising their emotions as valid, normal, and manageable, and providing an environment in which children feel safe to express their feelings (Gottman & DeClaire, 1998).

5.4 Parenting to Promote Pro-Environmental Values

There is a growing literature on the vital role that parents play in promoting pro-environmental values in children from early in their lives. By adulthood, people have often formed deeply entrenched attitudes and behaviours which are resistant to change. Understanding the factors in childhood which facilitate the development of pro-environmental attitudes and behaviours can help to ensure that children are prepared to engage in the wide-ranging behavioural changes that are needed to restore a safe climate.

Research on the childhood origins of pro-environmental values and behaviours have identified a number of roles for parents. Key factors are parents' own environmental attitudes and behaviours and giving children time in nature. In the first longitudinal study of children's environmental attitudes and behaviours, Evans et al. (2018) looked at children at age seven years and followed up at age eighteen years to identify childhood factors related to pro-environmental behaviour in young adulthood. They found that children whose mothers[8] had more pro-environmental attitudes and behaviours and provided children with opportunities to spend time in nature were themselves more engaged in pro-environmental behaviour as young adults. They also reported that the children's pro-environmental attitudes followed a ∩-shaped curve: increasing from seven to ten years, remaining level until age fourteen, then decreasing from fourteen to eighteen years. Other retrospective, correlational studies have reported a positive relation between active nature engagement (especially unstructured experiences) as a child and adult environmental behaviour and environmental citizenship (Hahn, 2021; Otto & Pensini, 2017). There is clearly a need for further longitudinal research on this issue with diverse samples of children.

Besides parental influence on their children, an interesting study by Lawson et al. (2019) showed that intergenerational learning can also occur from child to parent. Concerns about climate change increased more among parents of children (ten to fourteen years) who took part in a two-year climate change curriculum (which included children interviewing their parents) compared to a control group, and this change was mediated by changes in children's climate concerns. The effects were strongest for politically conservative fathers.

---

[8] Fathers didn't participate in this study. Maternal education was also a positive predictor.

The benefits of climate change education are discussed in further detail in the following section.

5.5 Time in Nature

Researchers examining the benefits of time spent in nature in childhood report a range of consequences. The benefits include children feeling more closely connected to nature and expressing a greater willingness to protect nature (Hahn, 2021) and perform sustainable behaviours (Barrera-Hernández et al., 2020). Other positive outcomes included greater levels of emotional and cognitive self-regulation, more prosocial behaviours, improved parent–child communication, cognitive benefits (Hahn, 2021), greater subjective well-being, happiness, health, creative thinking, attention, resilience and benefits to physical and mental health (Chawla, 2020; Tillman et al., 2018).

Chawla's (2020) review noted some specific parent/adult factors that contributed to children's connecting to nature, including a nurturing parenting style, adults promoting engagement with nature and empathy for living things, pro-environmental family styles, and living within families/communities upholding Indigenous values of care for nature, or sustainable practices of living on the land. Green (2018) used the term 'natural world socialisation' to refer to the process by which parents can nurture nature connection in toddlers and younger children by keeping a child safe while allowing independent exploration and appropriate risk taking, appreciating the child's accomplishments and discoveries, and promoting care for the environment. These parenting practices all help to build the young child's pro-environmental values and behaviours (Chawla & Derr, 2012; Sobel, 2008). With older children, this *hands-on/hands-off* approach can be adopted not just by parents, but by other adults and peers who accompany or facilitate children's time in nature. Louv (2021), a nature educator and writer, argued that parents can and should choose to spend more time with children in nature, making it an everyday event.

Farming, herding, hunting, and foraging families who want to maintain productive lands need to conserve the use of natural resources and actively teach this to their children. Marin and Bang (2018) described how Native American (Menominee) parents cultivated a particular way of perceiving nature during outdoor activities with their children (e.g., forest walks, berry picking, fishing, hunting, harvesting medicinal plants), actively emphasising care for nature as an important value, using terms like 'Mother Earth', talking about the environment as an extended community where humans are only one of many members, and teaching them to observe closely and notice interdependencies among species (Bang et al., 2015).

Allowing children time to connect with nature, whether as recreation or livelihood, as well as parental values and attitudes, family norms, and conversations, are all clearly significant factors influencing children's pro-environmentalism, and are critical for building children's capacity to care for the planet and hence for their own future.

5.6 Parents in Action – Mitigating and Modelling

In the Global Action report (Global Action Plan UK & Unilever, 2021), many parents acknowledged the importance of taking action on the issues facing the world, but many (60 per cent) also acknowledged that they themselves were not doing enough. Parents were actually more optimistic about the potential of the younger generation to bring about positive change, with 73 per cent believing their child can make the changes their generation has not been able to make. Unfortunately, this deferral of responsibility for solving the climate crisis to young people is not fair, too slow, and harmful to children.

Cripps (2017) argued that today's parents have a moral duty to protect their children's interests by engaging in climate adaptation and mitigation behaviours themselves. This parental duty arises because parents caused their child 'to exist in a condition of vulnerability' and because parents have 'implicitly or explicitly committed to caring for their child' (p. 13). Although creating the conditions to allow the next generation to flourish may be the primary responsibility of the State or the general population, when this responsibility is not fulfilled, parents must act instead. Cripps emphasised that this duty applies especially to relatively affluent parents who have more power to take action. Importantly, she noted that parents today may be the last generation who can actually do anything about managing the climate crisis – it will be too late for the next generation to act. Similarly, Eklund and Nylén (2021), in the *OurKidsClimate* parenting tipsheet, argued that as adults today have created the crisis, adults must lead the way in resolving it. Equally critical is to demonstrate to young people that they are not being asked to take the whole burden for action on climate change themselves (Sanson & Bellemo, 2021).

The researchers in the aforementioned Global Action study argued that parents need to be seen by young people to be taking action because young people are already worried about these issues and they perceive adults' lack of engagement with climate change as a lack of concern. About one-half of the young people surveyed thought that caring for nature was 'not important' to adults and more than one-half thought that only a 'few people' or 'no one' where they lived did things to help the natural world. Similarly, Hickman et al. (2021), in their study of 10,000 youth, found that 85 per cent believed that people had failed to care for the planet. This finding suggests that young people are pessimistic about the extent to which adults care about nature and, by extension, about their own future lives. Also, when young people think that others are not taking care, they are less likely to engage in pro-environmental behaviours themselves. Parents as role models of action on the climate crisis can help children and young people believe that the adults around them are caring, and actually 'doing something', thereby building their sense of optimism and well-being as well as helping to foster their own compassionate values and their confidence and motivation to act themselves (Global Action Plan UK & Unilever, 2021).

A key factor that contributes to climate anxiety is knowing that danger is approaching but not having any appropriate scripts, skills, or direct agency in place to mitigate it (Ingle & Mikulewicz, 2020). When parents engage with children's concerns about environmental issues, encourage them to explore ways to take action on the problem that is distressing them, and respond in solution-oriented and supportive ways (rather than being dismissive or voices of doom and gloom), then children are more likely to use constructive coping strategies (Ojala & Bengtsson, 2019).

Furthermore, the Global Action research indicates that young people actually want parents to take action with them, as illustrated by Ellen (aged fourteen to sixteen years): 'Go with them and protest with them. See what goes on and then go from there' (Global Action Plan UK & Unilever, 2021, p. 34). In Section 6, we provide further examples of climate projects that children and parents can work on together.

5.7 Preparing Parents for the Challenge of Parenting in the Age of Climate Change

An exponential increase in parent climate groups in the Global North and Global South (e.g., Parents for Future; Our Kids Climate; Australian Parents for Climate Action) and increasing numbers of families at climate rallies around the world indicate widespread parental concern about the impact of the climate crisis on their children. Despite these examples, there exists little systematic research to date on how parents perceive the threat of climate change and its impact on their children, and how they cope with that knowledge themselves, including overcoming psychological barriers to engaging with it (APS, 2017; Gifford, 2011; see also discussion in Section 1). Helping parents to cope with their own climate distress is critical in helping them to engage with their children, but again there is no research on how to do this effectively. Some psychological support groups have emerged in the Global North to help people come to terms with their climate distress (e.g., Good Grief Network; Psychology for a Safe Climate; Climate Grief

Groups); however, these groups generally reach very small numbers of people. We are aware of no research on whether or how parents (per se) adopt helpful strategies or could be supported to do so. This is clearly an area in need of research.

Finally, there is evidence that many young people question whether to become parents themselves because of their grave concerns about the climate crisis. One in three Australian women in the under-thirty age bracket surveyed by the Australian Conservation Foundation and One Million Women (2019) reported being hesitant to have children due to climate change.

5.8 Concluding Section Comments

Parents are tasked with a big job in preparing children in the current global environment in which they must survive and, hopefully, thrive (Bornstein, 2015). They have to face the reality that their children, and their children's children, may inherit an unlivable planet unless there is urgent action. Given this unprecedented situation, it is understandable that many parents are anxious about how to rear their children through the climate crisis. It is shocking that so little research has been conducted on how parents approach this vital responsibility and how they can be supported to do so effectively.

For parents living in areas where climate change is still largely a future threat, the task of preparing children for a climate-changed world is critically important. This task has greater urgency for families living in geographically vulnerable areas where parents need to help children prepare for and recover from the direct impacts of climate change, as well as cope with long-term climate change like droughts and sea level rise. However, this important task will be increasingly true for parents worldwide as climate impacts escalate. Wherever they live, parents share a special duty to protect their children and their children's interests. In today's world, that responsibility entails seriously engaging with the urgent problem of climate crisis.

6 Climate Change Education

Today's children are growing up in a rapidly changing world shaped by climate change. Hence, today's educators confront an unprecedented situation where they are preparing students for a dangerous and uncertain future. The Convention on the Rights of the Child asserts children's right to know about things that will affect their future and be involved in decision-making about them (UN, 1989). The goal of climate change education is to provide learners with the knowledge, attitudes, and abilities they will need to respond effectively to present and future climate challenges and avoid future climate catastrophe.

Effective climate change education is multi-dimensional and integrates emotional, cognitive, and social aspects. Furthermore, as Reid (2019) emphasised, 'climate change education' is not simply 'climate education' but must have strong action orientations.

UN CC: Learn (2013, p. 4), a partnership of UNICEF, United Nations Educational, Scientific and Cultural Organization [UNESCO], and numerous other organisations, provides this useful definition:

> [Climate change education] promotes learning about the causes and effects of climate change as well as possible responses, providing a cross-curricular and multi-disciplinary perspective. It develops competences in the field of climate change mitigation and adaptation, with the aim to promote climate-resilient development and reduce the vulnerability of communities in the face of an uncertain future. Additionally, by preparing learners, communities and education systems to face natural hazards, [it] contributes to disaster risk reduction efforts. Finally, [it] helps individuals to make informed decisions and highlights links between consumption patterns and climate change in order to mobilise responsible actions contributing to reduced greenhouse gas emissions through more sustainable lifestyles.

In this section, we consider 'education' in the broad sense that includes both *formal* and *informal* education. When we think of *formal* education, we usually think of schools, but in fact it involves the entire educational system including governance, curriculum, assessments, and so forth, from preschool through to university and beyond. *Informal* education refers to the varied experiences that children have outside the classroom, in settings ranging from interactions with family, peers, and members of their communities, to explorations and play in neighbourhood parks, to experiences with diverse media.

6.1 Integrating Climate Change Education: A Global Challenge

Climate change education is challenging to implement but essential for students. Many countries now integrate climate change education into the national curriculum; however, even with widespread public and political support, countries face daunting challenges. One such challenge is that many students face increased disruptions in their schooling due to climate change.

The 2021 UNESCO report *Learn for Our Planet* presented findings from an analysis of educational plans and curricula frameworks in about fifty countries globally. More than half still made no reference to climate change. Furthermore, the report noted the lack of attention to the critical socio-emotional skills and action-oriented competencies central to environmental and climate action. An online survey of 1,600 teachers and education leaders conducted for the report found that one-third of respondents reported that environment-related issues were not part of their training. UNESCO has set 2025 as the ambitious target to make environmental education a core curriculum component globally.

UNESCO, UNICEF, and The One UN Climate Change Learning Partnership have a wealth of projects, training, and other resources available on their websites to assist countries and educators in implementing climate change education in schools as well as ideas and resources for informal climate change education in families and communities.

6.2 Climate Change Education for Children

Because the purpose of climate change education is to promote students' knowledge, concern, hope, and ability to act, educators and scientists emphasise the importance of including climate change education in the earlier years when children's values, feelings, and attitudes are forming. Thereafter, climate change education should be integrated across the curriculum in age-appropriate ways throughout middle childhood, adolescence, young adulthood, and beyond.

Before turning to specific studies, we summarise findings from three reviews of climate change education for children and youth, usually through to age twenty-four years. First, Rousell and Cutter-Mackenzie-Knowles (2019) reviewed 221 articles published from 1993 to 2014 that included both formal and informal education settings. Studies varied greatly across countries and regions. About a one-third were from the USA and focused on formal science curricula in schools and universities. Studies from Canada and Europe included pedagogical and social initiatives. The authors found ten to twelve publications each from Africa and Australia but few studies from Asia and South America. In the greatly impacted Pacific Islands, climate change education was notably practical, focusing on adaptation and mitigation of disaster risks such as rising sea levels. Rousell and Cutter-Mackenzie-Knowles concluded that most programs focus solely on knowledge about climate change and emphasised the need for future approaches that support students' social, emotional, and creative development in addition to their knowledge.

The purpose of the review by Monroe et al. (2019) was to identify effective climate change education strategies as measured by program assessments as well as innovations to inform future programs. Of the 959 publications reviewed, only 49 included assessments. Of these, only nine included children in primary grades. Monroe and colleagues highlighted two strategies that consistently increased program success for learners of all ages: a focus on making climate change education personally relevant and meaningful for learners and inclusion of educational activities or interventions designed to engage learners. Others have found that the following additional characteristics contribute to success: whole school interdisciplinary approaches; a school culture of sustainability; emphasis on social and emotional dimensions of learning; group discussions that help learners understand different viewpoints and gain knowledge about climate change; and opportunities for learners to design and implement school or community projects and actions. To these we would add: the inclusion of a global as well as local focus and the integration of a global climate justice approach. These characteristics mirror many that UNESCO (2021) identified. But the question remains: How common is this approach to learning? The answer is: Not very – as UNESCO found.

A third review by Apollo and Mbah (2021) focused specifically on East African countries, all of which are largely agro-pastoral and greatly impacted by climate change. However, Apollo and Mbah noted that countries in East Africa have significant opportunities to implement climate change education because of wide support from educators and governments, and the presence of Indigenous knowledge systems. First, research shows that most teachers in these countries think that climate change education should be taught in schools and should promote students' actions and official policies to deal with the climate crisis (see Ochieng & Koske, 2013). Second, most East African governments are committed to providing educators with resources to integrate climate change education into their curricula. For example, Rwanda's Environmental Education for Sustainable Development strategy aims to create environmental awareness and foster eco-friendly attitudes by implementing ecological topics in all K-12 curricula (Muhirwa, 2020). Third, Indigenous knowledge systems, historically discounted as 'unscientific' partly due to colonialism, are now being embraced. For example, Songok et al. (2011) found that even farmers with a formal education currently consult Indigenous forecasts to plan their farming practices.

6.3 Climate Change Education for Children in Primary Schools

Educators in primary schools can foster children's active engagement and make climate change education personally relevant. What might childhood climate change education look like in the lower primary grades?

Fuyani works for the EarthChild Project (Druckerman, 2021). As an Xhosa growing up during Apartheid, she knew first-hand about the racial disparities in children's access to nature and became determined to share her love of nature: '[Children in marginalised communities are] already experiencing the effects of climate change and living in the future that many fear' (p. 121). Fuyani decided to develop a project that would be fun for young children and address a problem they confronted every day. Knowing that most of the children lived in shacks in informal settlements where waste management was a constant problem, she developed a curriculum to promote composting that involved worm farms to encourage children to learn about waste disposal, take responsibility for living things, develop self-sufficiency, and realise that they could grow food instead of just going to the store.

> We don't mention the words 'climate change' to 5-year-olds, but we do use local environmental issues to teach them about our planet. Young kids often ask, 'What can we do?' Having a worm farm in their classrooms shows that they are stopping organic waste from going into landfill sites. We try to stimulate their curiosity and teach creative problem solving and reflection. (p. 122)

This highly successful program serves hundreds of lower-grade primary students in Cape Town.

There is considerable literature on how educators in the upper primary grades can foster children's active engagement and make climate change education personally relevant. For example, Grumbach (2019) taught a climate change education unit to fifth grade students in Rhode Island, USA. She emphasised how important it was to anticipate and respond to students' feelings and promote their sense of hopefulness. '[T]o limit that general anxiety, we made sure to introduce our framing, driving question by the end of class. ... We highlighted the agency and impact of individual citizens and reassured them that, by the end of the unit, their minds would be brimming with possible answers to this question'. (pp. 36–37)

At the start, students investigated this personally relevant, action-oriented problem: *How can we, as fifth graders, help address the problems that are happening today in Rhode Island due to climate change?* They began by sharing what they had previously heard and their feelings about climate change. They then watched a video that showed observable impacts of climate change in their state and participated in activities to address their questions and gaps in their knowledge. The next lessons addressed the central question: *Why is the climate changing?* Children learned more through a mix of hands-on activities, teacher demonstrations, and videos that informed and empowered. At the end of the unit, Grumbach challenged students to take what they learned and develop projects to inform others at local or state levels. Their projects served as assessments and were highly successful. For example, students wrote to the principal asking that green roofs be installed on school buildings, wrote letters to the governor asking that only LED light bulbs be used in state buildings, and presented their ideas in a regional conference for educators.

Karpudewan et al. (2015) carried out a study with Malaysian fifth-year school students in which they compared the effects of a child-centred, active learning, inquiry-based approach to the more traditional teacher-centred curricula found in many schools. They then assessed children's knowledge about global warming and environmental attitudes and found statistically significant differences in favour of the group that participated in an active learning, inquiry-based approach with respect to both their knowledge and positive changes in their environmental attitudes. Interviews with randomly selected students from both groups further confirmed these findings.

6.4 Informal Climate Change Education

Informal climate change education can occur anywhere in children's environments, with opportunities provided by local and national governments, international and local organisations, and educators. (Section 4 provides suggestions for informal educational activities that families enjoy.)

The Bernard van Leer Foundation (2021) publication, *Caring for Children and the Planet*, described the many ways countries and communities worldwide are expanding children's opportunities to deepen their love of nature, a central goal of climate change education for young children. For example, the government of Udaipur, India, mapped the city to discover how well the city environment met the needs of infants, toddlers, and caregivers. The government implemented projects to expand green spaces where infants and toddlers could roam, touch and smell the plants, and feel the earth. Related measures to calm traffic helped the city adapt to climate change by reducing levels of CO_2 (The Bernard van Leer Foundation, 2021). In Addis Ababa, a major early childhood initiative supports children's connections with nature as an integral part of a plan for comprehensive child services (The Bernard van Leer Foundation, 2021). In Lima, Peru, the project *Limeños al Bicentenario* has turned concrete spaces that contribute to heatwaves and pollution into inviting green areas and parks that are accessible for people with disabilities and attract children, families, and elders to socialise, play, and breathe clean air (The Bernard van Leer Foundation, 2021).

Schools in some countries offer extra-curricular, after-school programs. *Science, Camera, Action*! (SCA) was an after-school, arts-based climate change education program for eleven- to twelve-year-old students in Colorado, USA. Trott (2019) designed the program expressly for children from low-income families who are often more seriously affected by climate change. She employed participatory research methods to promote children's sense of agency. Students were given cameras and asked to take photos that expressed their personal connections with community problems. They took hundreds of photos and excitedly discussed their photos' content and personal meaning. Trott used photovoice to capture the discussions. Dominic, age ten, described her experience: 'When we were first coming here, I [thought] it was going to be cool because of the pictures, and then we got into a new conversation [about] the planet, the plants, and how to save the world' (p. 51).

The children worked in groups that collaboratively planned and carried out successful action programs. For example, one group displayed their photovoice recordings at a well-attended gallery show and developed a popular SCA! website. Another carried out a tree-planting campaign and made a presentation to the city council which then presented the group with a commemorative plaque in recognition of their leadership. Despite increasing their awareness of climate risks, participation in the program promoted children's hope and well-being by helping them feel part of a collaborative effort. Participation gave them a sense of accomplishment and a stronger belief in their capabilities to remedy environmental problems through their own behaviours and decisions. Trott argued, therefore, that children's sense of agency was closely related to their perceived self- and collective efficacy and was a mixture of hope, confidence, and motivation to effect change.

Nature camps are popular for children in many countries. One example was the nature-based summer camp on the Greek island of Skyros implemented by a nearby university for two summers. Most campers were aged eleven years or younger. Skanavis and Kounani (2018) assessed the impact of the camp experience on children's climate change knowledge, attitudes, and willingness to act. Pre-camp assessments showed that children had learned most of what they knew about the environment at school. Comparison of pre- and post-camp assessments revealed that attending the camp made a difference. For example, at the start of camp, the great majority agreed with the statements that climate change is occurring and that everyone must do something to stop it, but every child answered that there was little they could do. By the end of the camp, 42 per cent of those who initially said that they had never participated in efforts to convince adults about climate change issues were now willing to try to do so and to work to reduce climate change.

Inventive and wide-ranging approaches to informal climate change education are being implemented worldwide by governments and agencies, NGOs, community groups, and individuals. In this way, informal education has great potential to engage children to act with others to address climate change.

6.5 Bridging Informal and Formal Approaches to Serve Children and Communities

The TiNi (ANIA ORG) and Sandwatch projects illustrate advantages of programs that can be implemented in both school and community settings. These names are descriptors. 'TiNi' literally means 'tiny': a 'TiNi' consists of a green or natural area that may be as small as half a square metre or much larger that is given solely to children to develop and care for. Similarly 'Sandwatch' projects involve local people watching sandy areas on beaches and riverbanks over time and working together to protect these environments. The goals of the TiNi methodology are for children to develop: (1) an emotional bond and empathy with the earth and living beings, (2) the knowledge and skills that allow them to adopt healthy and sustainable lifestyles, and (3) a sense of purpose knowing they are agents of change whose decisions and actions contribute to their well-being, and that of other people and nature. Children learn to grow food, medicinal plants, and pollinators on their TiNi, care for beneficial trees and habitats for animals, reuse water and solid waste, value their culture and identity, and express their feelings through art. Originally developed in Peru, the TiNi methodology has been implemented in more than ten countries, involving more than two million young people in restoring and caring for more than 2.5 million square metres of green and natural spaces. In 2012, UNESCO recognised the TiNi methodology as a good model of Education for Sustainable Development (ESD). TiNi is coordinated by the Association for Children and their Environment (ANIA ORG).

Like TiNi, Sandwatch is implemented in formal and informal educational settings to help children, young people, and families develop the attitudes, knowledge, and agency they need to protect their environment – in this case, beaches and sandy riverbanks. Examples of local projects include restoring dunes and planting native grasses to reduce erosion. Sandwatch was first developed in Puerto Rico, then sponsored by UNESCO. Today the Sandwatch Foundation coordinates a worldwide network of programs in schools and communities. More than fifty countries formally participate in the Sandwatch program.

6.6 Concluding Section Comments

The need for universal action-oriented climate change education is articulated well by Kagawa and Selby (2010, pp. 4–5): 'The accelerating climate crisis impacting life on the planet demands increasing knowledge, concern, and action by a knowledgeable and active populace around the globe to collectively envision a better future, and then to become practical visionaries in realising that future'. Climate change is a complex concept that takes time to fully understand, not one that children grasp all at once but one that children can learn in culturally and developmentally appropriate ways throughout childhood. Furthermore, as climate scientists point out, climate change is a rapidly growing field of study which means that we must all become lifetime learners.

Can effective climate change education help provide current and future generations with the knowledge, attitudes, and agency to help them realise more liveable futures? The evidence shows that more countries are including climate change education in their national curricula. However, although this is an important step, in most countries there is insufficient social and political will to provide adequate funding to implement effective policies, train teachers, and provide resources. Many resources exist but very many more are needed across the curricula and throughout communities. Multidisciplinary collaborations and funding are needed to design and implement creative, culturally and age-appropriate approaches to effective climate change education.

7 Preparing Children for the World They Will Inherit as Adults

Sections 5 and 6 focused largely on how best to support children in the here and now. This section takes a longer-term focus and considers how best to prepare children for what lies ahead. We cannot see into the future, but it is reasonable to forecast that the current generation of children will experience more change over their lifetimes than any previous generation. Some of this change will be due to the disruptive effects of climate change itself, and some will be from fast and large-scale societal changes that will occur in attempts to mitigate and adapt to it.

First, the IPCC (2021) noted that, even with strong and sustained reductions in greenhouse gas emissions, it could take twenty to thirty years for global temperatures to stabilise due to the high atmospheric concentration of greenhouse gases and other climate effects already locked-in (Steffen et al., 2018). As shown by Thiery et al. (2021), even with warming limited to 1.5°C, the next generation will still have unprecedented exposure to extreme climate-induced events. Over their lifetimes, they will thus experience a world of more frequent and severe extreme weather events – heatwaves, fires, floods, hurricanes – along with slower effects such as droughts, rising sea levels, and ocean acidification. Many millions of climate refugees are predicted. Massive migrations, along with food and water scarcity, will create potent conditions for intrastate and interstate conflict (UN News, 2019). In terms of the natural environment, more rapid extinctions of plants and animals are predicted. With slower global action, impacts will be worse and may lead to irreversible changes. As pointed out by UNICEF (2021a, p. 10),

'The world's children ... must make their way in a world that will become far more dangerous and uncertain in the years to come' (p. 10).

At the same time, the transition to a zero-carbon economy – a necessity for humankind's survival – will also entail considerable and rapid change in many aspects of life, including how we protect nature, how we produce and use energy, how we work, how we get from place to place, and how we grow and use food. As described in *Nature* (2021, p. 386),

> Replacing fossil fuels is one section (although admittedly a large one) of a thousand-piece jigsaw. The scale of the net-zero challenge is like nothing that has come before. Tackling global warming requires a revolution in how economies are run, and in the choices world leaders must make. Energy and industry, agriculture, financial services, transport and much more must be transformed. Natural ecosystems that absorb carbon emissions need protection.

Hence, due to both climate effects and mitigation efforts, the next generation will need to adapt to fast and wide-ranging changes. Here we consider the attributes and competencies that will help them to adapt successfully to these challenges. We argue that many of these 'survival skills' have their roots in early and middle childhood and therefore should be a focus in our efforts to prepare the next generation for their lives ahead. The provision of these skills involves both parenting and education, as well as communities and society more broadly.

In considering the attributes that the next generation of young people will need, we draw on the literature on resilience and positive development. These overlap to a considerable extent, but each offers unique insights. Resilience research typically adopts a developmental systems approach (Masten, 2021) or, more broadly, a socio-ecological developmental systems approach (Schoon, 2021). From these perspectives, the capacity for resilience (adapting to challenging circumstances) takes into account the characteristics of the individual as well as the individual's interactions and connections to many other systems or contexts, including the family, school, peer groups, community, culture, and natural environment. The resilience of an individual child thus depends on the resilience of other systems. Resilience develops over time. Risk effects appear to be strongest during infancy, preschool, and the early school years, but childhood is also an important period for nurturing the resilience to face future challenges, both for individuals and societies.

Resilience-promoting factors commonly identified in the literature include the following: social connectedness; sense of belonging; optimism or a positive outlook; meaning; agency; self-efficacy and collective efficacy; problem-solving skills; and executive function and leadership skills. Children's families, schools, communities, cultures, and religions can nurture resilience in children by modelling, teaching, and otherwise fostering the development of supportive relationships, problem-solving skills, self-regulation skills, agency, and a sense of belonging (Masten, 2014, 2018).

Models of positive development (e.g., Hawkins et al., 2009; Lerner et al., 2005; Masten & Cicchetti, 2016; Petersen et al., 2017) vary in their specifics but share a number of commonalities. They all emphasise competence in: (1) individual-level attributes such as flexibility and adaptability; self-regulation, self-esteem, and self-efficacy; and self-transcendent values such as empathy, love of nature, and beliefs in justice and equity; (2) interpersonal spheres, reflected in healthy relationships with parents, peers, and others, and the capacity to cooperate and negotiate with others; and (3) at the community/social level, attributes such as community involvement, citizenship skills, and trust and tolerance of others (APS, 2018b; Sanson & Burke, 2019).

There is considerable overlap between individual-level positive developmental attributes and the resilience-promoting factors identified by Masten (2021), but positive development gives greater weight to interpersonal and community competencies. In this it is similar to the construct of global citizenship, conceptualised to include three interrelated dimensions: social responsibility (e.g., concern over global justice, altruism, and an ethic of social service), global competence (e.g., intercultural communication skills, and interest in world issues), and global civic engagement (e.g., involvement in civic organisations, and civic activism to advance global agendas; Anthony et al., 2014; Morais & Ogden, 2011). Many of these positive development and global citizenship attributes reflect the Aristotelian concept of *eudaimonia* (realising human potential through meaningful living) in contrast to *hedonia* (or pleasure-seeking) and provide foundational capacities for adaptation in the face of the changes ahead. For example, to maintain peace in the face of climate-induced disruptions such as resource shortages, increased inequality, and major migrations, young people will need skills in conflict resolution, problem-solving, intercultural understanding, empathy and acceptance, and beliefs in environmental protection, equality, and justice (Sanson & Burke, 2019). To deal effectively with the move to a zero-carbon and more localised world will require skills in cooperation, trust towards others, a strong community orientation, and civic engagement.

Resilience, positive development, and global citizenship are characteristics typically studied in adolescence and adulthood. However, the literatures on both resilience and positive development emphasise the importance of earlier phases of life in developing these attributes. For example, O'Connor et al. (2011) showed that positive development in late adolescence and early adulthood

was predicted by four broad factors from childhood through early adolescence, ranging from individual characteristics to micro-, meso-, and exosystem influences: (1) the capacity to self-regulate feelings, attention, and
behaviour; (2) positive and supportive relationships with parents, peers, and
teachers; (3) school connectedness (the child's feeling that school recognises
and values them); and (4) being a contributing member of their community
(including joining groups, volunteering, and being interested in political
issues).

7.1 Concluding Section Comments

Efforts by parents, teachers, and others are clearly vital in helping children to
not only cope in the here and now but also to be well-prepared for responding
adaptively to future climate-related changes. There is considerable overlap
between the strategies to achieve these two goals (current coping and future
preparedness), but strategies of particular importance for the longer term might
include helping children learn to delay gratification and build the capacity to
work towards long-term goals (e.g., teaching the importance of acting to reduce
emissions now for positive effects on global temperatures in the future); parents
and teachers recognising the critical importance of maintaining positive supportive relationships with children even when the going gets tough; social skills
training for children to build their capacity to make and maintain strong
relationships to help them cope with future climate disruptions; schools ensuring that their curricula feel relevant to children by covering the causes, future
impacts, and most importantly the solutions to the climate crisis; encouraging
small-scale volunteering with other children such as planting trees and community gardens and helping neighbours; engaging children in conversations and in
formal education about the future they envisage and the world beyond their
immediate contexts; and supporting them if they want to undertake more
activist roles.

An important caveat to this discussion relates to the paucity of research on the
concepts of positive development and resilience to climate disruption in the
Global South. Almost all the relevant research has been conducted in wealthy
Western countries. Contributors to Petersen et al.'s (2017) book, *Positive Youth
Development in Global Contexts of Social and Economic Change* provide some
useful directions, but virtually no work has taken a developmental perspective
covering the childhood years, and it is still uncertain how applicable these
concepts are for the non-Western countries in the Global South which will
continue to bear the brunt of climate change. Importantly, it is crucial that
researchers in the Global South receive the necessary support to investigate

what is most useful and beneficial to children and families in these regions. This is clearly an important area for future research.

8 Conclusions, Future Directions, and a Call to Action

The preceding sections have documented the many ways in which the climate crisis is a defining issue for the children of today and tomorrow, and hence also for those with concern and responsibility for their healthy development. As noted by UNICEF (2021a, p. 117), climate change is 'one of the most intersectional challenges in history, having its causes and impacts deeply embedded in wider systems that also shape economic and social inequality'. Hence an analysis of its impacts on children needs to take a broad perspective, looking at all the systems affecting a child's development, from their own characteristics through to the broadest societal level. We have attempted to address this breadth in our coverage of the existing literature through the adoption of a bioecological model based on Bronfenbrenner's work. Furthermore, given that children in the Global South are even more vulnerable to climate change than those in the Global North, we have focused on this region as much as the scanty available research has allowed.

8.1 Review Implications

Section 2 presented clear evidence of children's greater vulnerability to climate change shocks, both the sudden catastrophes of extreme weather events and more insidious changes such as increasing temperatures, sea level rise, and long-lasting droughts. The evidence shows that most children globally are at risk of impacts ranging from death and serious injury to diseases and mental health conditions such as PTSD, as well as more indirect but equally damaging consequences such as malnutrition, forced migration, and disruptions to education. According to UNICEF (2021a), nearly half of the world's children (one billion children, mostly in the Global South) live in countries that are at 'extremely high-risk' from the impacts of climate change. Along with these global risks, we noted the particular vulnerabilities of groups such as girls, children with disabilities, children with socio-economic disadvantages including those living in slums, and children who belong to Indigenous and ethnic minority communities. Any deprivation as a result of climate and environmental degradation at a young age can result in a lifetime of lost opportunity (UNICEF, 2021a). Hence, as climate impacts continue to escalate rapidly, and more and more children are exposed to them, the protection of children's healthy development must be an issue of the highest concern.

Section 3 outlined the current evidence on children's knowledge about climate change and their emotional responses to that knowledge. Here we first encounter the problematic dearth of research on young children, and the near absence of systematic research on children in the Global South, problems which recur throughout our review. Most evidence from the Global South comes from reports from intergovernmental organisations and NGOs which tend to focus on impacts on children's physical and social well-being and their educational opportunities, and highlight actions that these agencies are taking to mitigate climate change locally or to help people adapt to it. Some tap children's knowledge of local climate impacts, but few assess their knowledge of the broader phenomenon of climate change. And few directly address children's emotional reactions to experiencing climate impacts.

Despite the scarcity of research, it is clear that most children have at least informal knowledge about the problematic climate-related changes in the environment around them and are concerned about how they will affect their future. The emotions identified in the available research and reports include feeling terrified, helpless, hopeless, worried, and exasperated that no one has helped them as well as grief and feelings of loss. Furthermore, large-scale surveys of adolescents across many countries show that a very high proportion are now seriously concerned about climate change – despite the lack of direct data, we can presume that for many, these concerns first emerged before adolescence. Growing up with fear for one's future, and senses of helplessness and hopelessness, is not conducive to healthy development.

Section 4 considered how children cope with climate change and the difficult feelings it raises. Once again, limited research has directly addressed this issue with young children, and virtually none in the Global South. However, a number of helpful coping strategies, as well as some less helpful ones, are identified. Being able to share their concerns, being supported to take action on the problem and develop a sense of agency and efficacy, spending time in nature, social support (including perceived support from noticing others are working on the problem), and learning about how other enormous challenges have been solved in the past, appear to be among the most helpful strategies. The need for more research on effective coping strategies for children of different ages and in different contexts is clearly indicated.

Today's parents are in an unprecedented situation, needing to nurture their children in the face of a potentially catastrophic future. Section 5 explored how parents can support their children in the era of climate crisis. Besides acknowledging their own emotional reactions to the crisis and finding ways to deal with them, a number of approaches for children across the age range of zero to twelve years are identified. Strategies include: spending time with children in nature, providing honest answers to children's questions, validating their feelings about the climate crisis, helping children notice, name, and manage feelings, modelling (and explaining) pro-environmental behaviours, engaging in their own climate actions, helping children think through how they can take action on the problem, and supporting them in their coping strategies and their actions.

Section 6 turned to the role of education, both formal and informal. Educators, like parents, face unprecedented challenges in supporting children facing climate disruptions and preparing them for an uncertain future. From a child's rights perspective, all children should receive accurate and appropriate information about climate change and be provided with the skills and training they need to contribute to addressing it. Effective climate change education supports children building their knowledge and taking actions at all ecological levels. It is multidimensional, integrating emotional and social as well as cognitive aspects. Our review identified some promising curricula and program initiatives in which educators and other adults acknowledged children's fears and, at the same time, promoted their hope and efficacy. Throughout both the Global North and Global South, however, climate change education is currently very patchy. As UNICEF (2021a, p. 24) concluded, 'Urgent action is needed to "climate proof" the education sector and to produce information that is accurate and empowers children to become climate-conscious citizens who are actively involved in climate adaptation and mitigation'.

Section 7 took a longer view, considering the attributes that children need to develop in the early years to cope well with the challenges that lie ahead of them – those brought about both by climate change itself and by the transformations in society that are needed to mitigate the crisis. It drew on positive development and resilience literature to identify relevant characteristics in three categories – individual attributes, interpersonal skills, and social and civic engagement. Evidence on the roots of these characteristics in earlier childhood can help guide parents, teachers, researchers, practitioners, and others in efforts to support children.

Table 1 draws from and partially summarises our review. It provides some illustrative examples of impacts at all levels in the bioecological model, both from experiencing extreme weather disasters and slower climate changes in the face of inadequate global action to mitigate the crisis. It also includes some of the conditions that will be needed for children to thrive, ranging from their own characteristics to policy changes and action at a global level. However, it is difficult to convey in a table the complex and often synergistic interactions among all these variables, some of which are graphically portrayed in Figure 1. While Table 1 does not pretend to be comprehensive, it does draw attention to

Table 1 Examples of impacts of the climate crisis on children across levels of the bioecological model (omitting critically important interactions among these)

System	1. Impacts of climate-induced extreme weather events and disasters	2. Impacts of ongoing climate change with inadequate global action	3. Requirements for child resilience and well-being
Direct impacts on child	• Deaths and injuries • Infectious and vector-borne diseases • Respiratory conditions • Malnutrition and diarrheal diseases • Mental health problems (PTSD, depression, anxiety) • Sleep problems • Cognitive/learning problems • Developmental delays	As for Column 1, plus: • Anxiety, fear • Anger, frustration, sense of betrayal • Helplessness, hopelessness, depression • Grief, loss	• Self-regulation and effective coping skills • Realistic/constructive/active hope • Skills in collaborating with others and solving conflicts • Self- and collective- efficacy • Skills in active citizenship
Microsystem	• Death of parents/family members • Parental absence, separation, injury, or ill health	As for Column 1, plus: • Anxiety among parents and teachers (often unvoiced) • Lack of attention to child voices	• Caregivers engaged in climate action • Reduced stress and disruptions • Increased caregiver availability • Caregivers responsive to child concerns

	• Disrupted parenting, stressed family members • Disrupted routines including at home and school • Disrupted peer support		• Re-established routines (at home, school) • Increased peer interactions and support
Mesosystem	• Lack of adequate food and water • Loss of housing • Increase in family violence, chaos etc.) • Forced migration or evacuation	As for Column 1, plus: • Children's voices not heard • Cascading stressors create child vulnerability and reduce life opportunities	• Parents, teachers, and community leaders engaged in climate action • Caregivers responsive to child concerns • Climate change education integral to school curricula at all levels • Adequate food and water
Exosystem	• Economic disruption • Resource scarcity • Destruction of community infrastructure (e.g., schools, hospitals) and utilities (e.g., electricity, water) • Stressed/overwhelmed education, health and social services	As for Column 1, plus: • Increasing media (and social media) coverage of climate disasters lead to increasing community anxiety, anger, and despair • Policies unresponsive to children's needs • Social unrest	• Mass movement to create change at speed and scale • More localised economies • Strengthened community cohesion • Shift away from consumerist values and lifestyles • Natural environment more valued and protected.

Table 1 (cont.)

System	1. Impacts of climate-induced extreme weather events and disasters	2. Impacts of ongoing climate change with inadequate global action	3. Requirements for child resilience and well-being
	• Increase in community violence • Reinforcement of existing social and economic vulnerabilities, inequalities and disparities		• Global inclusion of climate change education in school curricula at all levels • Speedy transition to below-zero emissions (renewable energy, new clean jobs, regenerative agriculture, carbon sequestration/drawdown, reforestation, etc.)
Macrosystem	• Increase in intra and interstate conflict • Destruction of national infrastructure • Destruction of natural environment • Reinforcement of existing economic and social disparities among peoples, nations, and regions.	As for Column 1, plus: • Increasing temperatures, rising sea levels, more intense and frequent disasters • Government inaction • Collapse of biodiversity • Increased risk of pandemics	• Climate emergency declared and acted on globally • Redistribution of resources to Global South • Reduced human, environmental, and financial costs from cascading climate change disasters • Increased climate stability leading to improved human and environmental health • Fewer climate-induced intra- and interstate conflicts

the intersectionality of the crisis we face and the corresponding whole-of-society response that is required.

All of us who are concerned about children's development and well-being also need to look after our own mental well-being. The facts of the climate crisis, such as those detailed in the latest IPCC (2021) report, are alarming for everyone; it can be argued that, if we do not feel some level of fear and grief, we are in denial (Psychology For A Safe Climate). Climate distress can be the motivation for taking action on the climate crisis on behalf of children but can be very difficult to bear. Organisations such as Psychology for a Safe Climate, the Climate Psychology Alliance, and the Good Grief Network provide resources which help deal with difficult emotional responses to the crisis, particularly through sharing them with others. We also need to draw on sources of hope and courage, as explored by Wiseman (2021). Among other sources of hope, he encouraged us to note how '[h]uman history is full of extraordinary stories of courageous collective action driving transformational change' (p. 29). Examples include the abolition of slavery, the triumph of the suffragists, and the overthrow of apartheid. Children also need to be told these stories of successful collective efficacy to develop their own active hope.

We are writing this Element during the COVID-19 pandemic. This pandemic has challenged all of us and caused massive suffering worldwide both directly and through the resultant economic upheaval. However, as Mackay's cartoon (Figure 2) illustrates, its implications are dwarfed in comparison to the climate crisis. We have nevertheless learned valuable lessons from the pandemic. On the positive side, we have learned that borders are permeable and largely irrelevant in a global crisis – a *global* perspective is needed; that politicians *can* listen to the science and take advice from scientists; that governments *can* make dramatic changes fast when they are motivated to do so; that when governments tell the truth to the people about the threats they are facing, most people listen, respond appropriately and become more trusting of government; that people *can* make rapid and dramatic changes in their own lifestyles; that in a crisis most people show compassion and cooperation; and (more directly relevant to children) parents and teachers have learned how to support children in facing a crisis. On the negative side, we have seen that: the Global North has monopolised resources (such as vaccines) to the detriment of the Global South; that marginalised people have often suffered most and been least supported; that health systems are easily overwhelmed in a crisis; that authoritarianism and xenophobic nationalism can easily arise; and that the balance between individual freedoms and communal well-being can be difficult to maintain. These lessons are all directly relevant to the climate crisis.

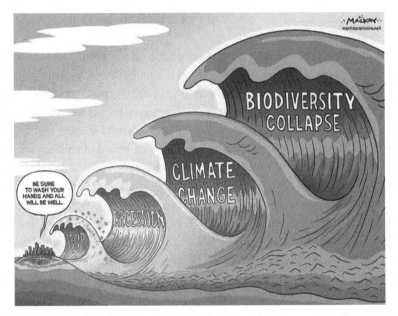

Figure 2 The impacts of the COVID-19 pandemic are swamped by those of climate change and the collapse of biodiversity. Reproduced with permission from Artizans Entertainment for Graeme MacKay

According to IPCC (2021), global greenhouse gas emissions need to be halved by 2030 and cut to zero by 2050 to avoid the worst climate impacts, but most countries are not on track to meet those targets. Transformative action is needed if we are to bequeath our children a livable planet. As Wiseman (2021, p. 70) noted, '"system change not climate change" will . . . be an essential precondition for the radical shift in economic, political and ecological values and relationships required to set the human project on a more sustainable path' (see also Newell et al., 2022). This review has underscored the importance of a sense of agency and action as a way for individual children to manage their climate anxiety. Hickman et al. (2021) reminded us that, to protect the mental health and well-being of all children and young people, action particularly needs to be taken by those in power, acknowledging children's rights, placing them at the centre of policy-making, and showing a commitment to ensuring their safe climate future.

The pandemic has offered an opportunity and underlined the necessity to make permanent positive political and economic changes to ensure a sustainable world, as articulated by UN Secretary General, Antonio Guterres in 2020'

> When we get past this crisis – which we will – we will face a choice. We can go back to the world as it was before or deal decisively with those issues that

make us all unnecessarily vulnerable to crises ... Everything we do during and after this crisis must be with a strong focus on building more equal, inclusive and sustainable economies and societies that are more resilient in the face of pandemics, climate change, and the many other global challenges we face (UN News, 2020).

Despite the efforts of those with vested interests in the *status quo* to protect their interests and resist change, those caring about the next generation can build on such statements in striving to create a healthy sustainable world for them.

8.2 Future Directions and a Call to Action

Overall, whether approaching the climate crisis from a child's rights perspective, as an issue of intergenerational justice and equity, or as a threat to children's health and development, it is clear that those with expertise in children's development, whether as professionals, educators, or researchers, face some unprecedented obligations. We argue that, if we are not handing over a livable planet to the next generation, other efforts to promote healthy child development are largely irrelevant. We need to recognise the unique situation that we are in, where 'business as usual' is not a viable option, and consider how we can reprioritise our work. Just as the climate crisis is creating multifarious threats, the ways in which we need to respond to it are also many and various. In the following section we outline some of these ways.

UNICEF (2021a) identified the countries where children are at most risk from climate change, which are predominantly in the Global South. It follows that these countries should be priority locations for research. Yet this review has shown how this is far from the case. Researchers need to ask why there are so few studies of children in the Global South and how this dearth can be remedied. Many more researchers work in the Global North than the Global South and receive far greater funding for their research. It is critical that researchers in the Global South receive adequate funding to conduct research. We also suggest that researchers in the Global North seek to develop collaborative, interdisciplinary, and culturally respectful partnerships with those in the Global South, perhaps working with international agencies, and lobby their funding bodies to support such research.

We have documented that young children are the most vulnerable to climate impacts, and can carry the negative consequences throughout their lives. Yet there is a paucity of research on them in comparison to adolescents and adults. There are understandable reasons for this pattern: for example, fewer rules govern consent for those over eighteen years; given their more limited language and conceptual skills, it is harder to assess young children's knowledge and responses about complex concepts like climate change; and convenient cheap methods of data collection such as on-line surveys are not appropriate for young children. Furthermore, some researchers may be hesitant to ask young children about issues that may raise fears and concerns. However, these obstacles can all be overcome, and increasing understanding of the impacts of the climate crisis on young children and how they can best be supported in all the contexts of their lives is critical.

Much research to date has taken an individualistic approach, for example simply identifying children's knowledge and concerns, without taking into account the many levels of influence on their health, knowledge, and development. It is important for researchers to adopt a broader perspective, such as the bioecological model presented here, to take account of what is happening in the child's family, school, community, and broader environment. We agree with Rousell and Cutter-Mackenzie-Knowles (2019) that we need to go beyond assessing levels of knowledge or concerns and focus on how children can best be supported to cope, adapt, and build a sense of efficacy and agency. As UNICEF (2021a, p. 117) put it, 'Every child and young person – 3.5 billion by 2030 – should be protected from the worst impacts of climate change and environmental degradation, as well as being part of the solution and the movement to heal the planet'. The report goes on to say 'It is time we provide all children and young people the resources they need and empower them as agents of change – to give them the best possible chance to address a crisis that we have bestowed upon them' (p. 118).

In undertaking more intervention research in this area, it is useful to consider the three basic intervention strategies that Masten (2021) identified to build resilience in the context of adversity. The first is preventing or mitigating risk, lowering the burden for resilience by reducing exposure to adversity. This is the most critical strategy in the context of climate change. In many contexts, children can be involved in disaster risk reduction initiatives (Back et al., 2009; Sanson, Burke, & Van Hoorn, 2018). More significantly, if we do not succeed in slowing the pace and lessening the extent of climate change, there will be little we can do to prevent massive suffering for children everywhere.

However, adoption of Masten's other two strategies is also necessary. The second strategy is boosting resources that support positive development of all children through actions ranging from cash transfers to childcare. Sections 5, 6, and 7 contain pointers to areas worthy of further development in this vein. The third strategy is to mobilise powerful adaptive systems that protect or drive positive adaptation in the context of adversity, such as fostering good caregiving and supportive relationships, strengthening self-regulation and problem-solving skills, and building self-efficacy. Masten identified several examples of global humanitarian efforts to promote positive development and flourishing among children and their families contending with or fleeing conditions of extreme poverty, violence, or marginalisation, which could help shape interventions in the context of climate change. There are important opportunities for researchers and practitioners to build, implement, and evaluate programs based on these strategies for children in specific contexts.

Parents need support in carrying out their roles in the face of the climate crisis, helping their children develop strong coping skills, values, and attributes that will stand them in good stead for the future. As noted in Section 5, some resources are available, and parent support groups are springing up (e.g., Parents for Future, Australian Parents for Climate Action). The experience of two of the authors (AS, SB) is that there is strong demand for parent training workshops on this issue, but insufficient numbers of professionals to run them. However, to our knowledge, no systematic research has been done to evaluate the effectiveness of particular approaches adopted by parents, for children of different ages, with different characteristics, and in different contexts. Here again, there is an urgent need for professionals to create programs to help parents develop competency and confidence to support their children as well as look after themselves, and for these to be carefully evaluated.

Teachers too need support. Some schools embrace climate change education, but they are in a minority, and many teachers struggle to overcome resistance in incorporating climate change into their teaching. Developmental scientists are in a strong position to work with educational institutions of all sorts to develop, implement, and evaluate curricula that fill the criteria discussed in Section 6. To overcome the senses of hopelessness and helplessness that children often feel, critical components of such education should be building children's global citizenship skills and their capacity to take action. Like parents, teachers should also be reminded that they are important role models to children and that children are very sensitive to hypocrisy. 'Practicing what you preach' by modelling environmentally aware behaviour and taking a stand on the climate crisis should be seen as part of their role.

Finally, all those caring for and about children's healthy development need to act as citizens at this time of urgency. Whatever our role, we have credibility, and can speak out for urgent action on climate change – within our own workplaces, professional organisations, and communities, as well as industries, corporations, and governments.

References

Akpan, N. (2019). *How to talk to your kids about climate change*. PBS Science. www.pbs.org/newshour/science/how-to-talk-to-your-kids-about-climate-change.

Akresh, R. (2016). Climate change, conflict, and children. *The Future of Children, 26*(1), 51–71. https://doi.org/10.1353/foc.2016.0003.

Albrecht, G., Sartore, G.-M., Connor, L. et al. (2007). Solastalgia: The distress caused by environmental change. *Australasian Psychiatry: Bulletin of Royal Australian and New Zealand College of Psychiatrists, 15 Suppl 1*, S95–S98. https://doi.org/10.1080/10398560701701288.

Alston, M., Whittenbury, K., Haynes, A., & Godden, N. (2014). Are climate challenges reinforcing child and forced marriage and dowry as adaptation strategies in the context of Bangladesh? *Women's Studies International Forum, 47*, 137–44. https://doi.org/10.1016/j.wsif.2014.08.005.

American Public Health Association (APHA). (2019). *Making the connection: Climate changes children's mental health*. https://apha.org/climate-changes-health.

Anderko, L., Du, M., & Hauptman, M. (2020). Climate changes reproductive and children's health: A review of risks, exposures, and impacts. *Pediatric Research, 87*(2), 414–9. https://doi.org/10.1038/s41390-019-0654-7.

Anthony, D., Miller, P. B., & Yarrish, K. K. (2014). An analysis of initial global citizenship in a liberal arts college in northeastern Pennsylvania. *Journal of International Education Research (JIER), 10*(1), 23–28. https://doi.org/10.19030/jier.v10i1.8346.

Apollo, A., & Mbah, M. F. (2021). Challenges and opportunities for climate change education (CCE) in East Africa: A critical review. *Climate, 9*(6), 93. https://doi.org/10.3390/cli9060093.

Australian Conservation Foundation, & One Million Women. (11 February 2019). New survey shows women will change their lives – and votes – for climate action. www.acf.org.au/women_will_change_their_lives_and_votes_for_climate_action.

Australian Psychological Society (APS). (2016). *Tips for talking with and helping children and young people cope after tragic events: Guidelines for parents, caregivers and teachers*. https://psychology.org.au/getmedia/a61fcf9d-dc4c-40f3-b94d-65995c85995b/helping-children-affected-tragic-events.pdf.

Australian Psychological Society. (2017). *The climate change empowerment handbook: Psychological strategies to tackle climate change*. https://psych

ology.org.au/getmedia/88ee1716-2604-44ce-b87a-ca0408dfaa12/climate-change-empowerment-handbook.pdf.

Australian Psychological Society. (2018a). *A guide for parents about the climate crisis*. Melbourne. www.psychology.org.au/getmedia/f7d0974d-4424-4d60-a7eb-cfa0431b6860/Parents-guide-climate-crisis.pdf.

Australian Psychological Society. (2018b). *Raising children to thrive in a climate changed world*. www.psychology.org.au/getmedia/e8cda6ca-ecfe-42c7-8538-492950bac8ba/Raising-children-climate.pdf.

Bang, M., Marin, A., Medin, D., & Washinawatok, K. (2015). Learning by observing, pitching in, and being in relations in the natural world. In M. Correa-Chávez, R. Mejía-Arauz, & B. Rogoff (Eds.), *Children learn by observing and contributing to family and community endeavors: A cultural paradigm* (Advances in Child Development and Behavior Vol. 49, pp. 303–13). Academic Press.

Back, E., Cameron, C., & Tanner, T. (2009). Children and disaster risk reduction. Taking stock and moving forward. *Children in a Changing Climate Coalition*. Brighton: Institute of Developmental Studies. https://www.preven tionweb.net/files/15093_12085ChildLedDRRTakingStock1.pdf

Barrera-Hernández, L., Sotelo-Castillo, M., Echeverría-Castro, S., & Tapia-Fonllem, C. (2020). Connectedness to nature: Its impact on sustainable behaviors and happiness in children. *Frontiers in Psychology*, *11*, 276. https://doi.org/10.3389/fpsyg.2020.00276.

Bell, J., Poushter, J., Fagan, M., & Huang, C. (14 September 2021). In response to climate change, citizens in advanced economies are willing to alter how they live and work. *Pew Research Center's Global Attitudes Project*. www .pewresearch.org/global/2021/09/14/in-response-to-climate-change-citizens-in-advanced-economies-are-willing-to-alter-how-they-live-and-work/.

Benoit, L., Thomas, I., & Martin, A. (2021). Review: Ecological awareness, anxiety, and actions among youth and their parents – A qualitative study of newspaper narratives. *Child and Adolescent Mental Health*, *27*(1), 47–58. https://doi.org/10.1111/camh.12514.

Bernard van Leer Foundation. (2021). *Early childhood matters: The climate issue. Caring for children and the planet*. Bernard van Leer Foundation.

Berse, K. (2017). Climate change from the lens of Malolos children: Perception, impact and adaptation. *Disaster Prevention and Management: An International Journal*, *26*(2), 217–29.

Biswas, A., Rahman, A., Mashreky, S., Rahman, F., & Dalal, K. (2010). Unintentional injuries and parental violence against children during flood: A study in rural Bangladesh. *Rural and Remote Health*, *10*(1), 1199.

Blakstad, M. M., & Smith, E. R. (2020). Climate change worsens global inequity in maternal nutrition. *The Lancet Planetary Health*, *4*(12), e547–8.

Bornstein, M. H. (2015). Children's parents. In R. M. Lerner (Ed), *Handbook of child psychology and developmental science.* (7th ed., Vol. 4, pp. 1–78). https://doi.org/10.1002/9781118963418.childpsy403

Bornstein, M. H. (2021). Introduction: The SARS-CoV-2 pandemic: Issues for families, parents, and children. In M. H. Bornstein (Ed.), *Psychological insights for understanding COVID-19 and families, parents, and children* (pp. 1–69). Routledge/Taylor & Francis Group.

Breuer, J., & Freud, S. (2001). Studies on hysteria. In J. Strachey (Ed. & Trans.), *The standard edition of the complete psychological works of Sigmund Freud* (Vol. 2, pp. 3–309). Hogarth Press. (Original work published in 1895.)

Bronfenbrenner, U., & Morris, P. A. (1998). The ecology of developmental processes. In W. Damon & R. M. Lerner (Eds.), *Handbook of child psychology. Theoretical models of human development* (5th ed., Vol. 1, pp. 993–1028). Wiley.

Bronfenbrenner, U., & Morris, P. (2006). The bioecological model of human development. In W. Damon & R. M. Lerner (Series Eds.) & R. M. Lerner (Vol. Ed.), *Handbook of child psychology. Theoretical models of human development* (6th ed., Vol. 1, pp. 793–828). Wiley. https://doi.org/10.1002/9780470147658.chpsy0114.

Burke, S., Sanson, A., & Van Hoorn, J. (2018). The psychological effects of climate change on children. *Current Psychiatry Reports, 20*(5), 1–8. http://doi.org/10.1007/s11920-018-0896-9.

Chawla, L. (2020). Childhood nature connection and constructive hope: A review of research on connecting with nature and coping with environmental loss. *People and Nature, 2*(3), 619–642. https://doi.org/10.1002/pan3.10128.

Chawla, L., & Derr, V. (2012). The development of conservation behaviors in childhood and youth. In S. Clayton (Ed.), *Oxford library of psychology: The Oxford handbook of environmental and conservation psychology* (Vol. 1, pp. 527–55). Oxford University Press. https://doi.org/10.1093/oxfordhb/9780199733026.013.0028.

Chhokar, K., Dua, S., Taylor, N., Boyes, E., & Stanisstreet, M. (2011). Indian secondary students' views about global warming: Beliefs about the usefulness of actions and willingness to act. *International Journal of Science and Mathematics Education, 9*(5), 1167–88. https://doi.org/10.1007/s10763-010-9254-z.

Clarke, A. T. (2006). Coping with interpersonal stress and psychosocial health among children and adolescents: A meta-analysis. *Journal of Youth and Adolescence, 35*(1), 11–24. https://doi.org/10.1007/s10964-005-9001-x.

Clayton, S. (2020). Climate anxiety: Psychological responses to climate change. *Journal of Anxiety Disorders, 74*, 102263. https://doi.org/10.1016/j.janxdis.2020.102263.

Clayton, S., Manning, C., Krygsman, K., & Speiser, M. (2017). *Mental health and our changing climate: Impacts, implications, and guidance.* American Psychological Association/ecoAmerica.https://www.apa.org/news/press/releases/2017/03/mental-health-climate.pdf

Coffey, Y., Bhullar, N., Durkin, J., Islam, M. S., & Usher, K. (2021). Understanding eco-anxiety: A systematic scoping review of current literature and identified knowledge gaps. *The Journal of Climate Change and Health*, *3*, 100047. https://doi.org/10.1016/j.joclim.2021.100047

Cohen, J., Agel, L., Barlow, M., Garfinkel, C. I., & White, I. (2021). Linking Arctic variability and change with extreme winter weather in the United States. *Science*, *373*(6559), 1116–21 https://10.1126/science.abi9167

Cripps, E. (2017). Do parents have a special duty to mitigate climate change? *Politics, Philosophy & Economics*, 16(3), 308–25. https://doi.org/10.1177/1470594X17709038

Cuevas-Parra, P. (2020). *'Talk less and act more, the world needs help': Children front and centre of climate action.* World Vision.www.wvi.org/publications/report/climate-change/talk-less-and-act-more-world-needs-help-children-front-and.

Cunsolo, A., Harper, S. L., Minor, K. et al. (2020). Ecological grief and anxiety: The start of a healthy response to climate change? *The Lancet Planetary Health*, *4*(7), e261–e263. https://doi.org/10.1016/S2542-5196(20)30144-3

Devonald, M., Jones, N., & Yadete, W. (2020). *'The first thing that I fear for my future is lack of rain and drought': Climate change and its impacts on adolescent capabilities in low- and middle-income countries.* Gender and Adolescence.

Dewi, L. P., & Dartanto, T. (2019). Natural disasters and girls vulnerability: Is child marriage a coping strategy of economic shocks in Indonesia? *Vulnerable Children and Youth Studies*, *14*(1), 24–35. https://doi.org/10.1080/17450128.2018.1546025

Dodds, J. (2021). The psychology of climate anxiety. *BJPsych Bulletin*, *45*(4), 222–6. https://doi.org/10.1192/bjb.2021.18

Druckerman, P. (2021). Interview with Xoli Fuyani: 'I firmly believe that we should engage with children when they are young'. In Bernard van Leer Foundation (Ed.), *Early childhood matters: The climate issue. Caring for children and the planet* (pp. 120–3). Bernard van Leer Foundation.

Earle, L. (2021). Climate change is forcing young children into high-risk urban slums. In Bernard van Leer Foundation, *Early childhood matters: The climate issue. Caring for children and the planet* (pp. 28–30).

Eklund, F., & Nylén, K. (2021). *Talk to children about the climate crisis: A guide for parents and other adults.* Our Kids Climate. https://media.ourkidsclimate.org/2021/06/Talk-about-climate-guide-for-parents-2021-06-01.pdf

Engdahl, I. (2015). Early childhood education for sustainability: The OMEP world project. *International Journal of Early Childhood, 47*(3), 347–66. https://doi.org/10.1007/s13158-015-0149-6

Escobar, L. (20 January 2021). *Normal life washed away in Guatemala hurricanes in late 2020 were a double blow to a country already reeling from the COVID-19 pandemic.* UNICEF [Press release]. www.unicef.org/lac/en/stor ies/normal-life-washed-away-in-guatemala

Evans, G. W., Otto, S., & Kaiser, F. G. (2018). Childhood origins of young adult environmental behavior. *Psychological Science, 29*(5),679–87. https://doi .org/10.1177/0956797617741894

Folkman, S. (2008). The case for positive emotions in the stress process. *Anxiety, Stress, and Coping, 21*(1), 3–14. https://doi.org/10.1080/1061580070 1740457

Full Option Science System (FOSS). (2017). *Taking FOSS outdoors.* Regents of the University of California.

Fuller, M. G., Cavanaugh, N., Green, S., & Duderstadt, K. (2021). Climate change and state of the science for children's health and environmental health equity. *Journal of Pediatric Health Care, 36*(1), 20–6. https://doi.org/ 10.1016/j.pedhc.2021.08.003

Gallay, E., Furlan Brighente, M., Flanagan, C., & Lowenstein, E. (2022). Place-based civic science-collective environmental action and solidarity for eco-resilience. *Child and Adolescent Mental Health, 27*(1), 39–46. https:// doi.org/10.1111/camh.1237

Gaziulusoy, A. İ. (2020). The experiences of parents raising children in times of climate change: Towards a caring research agenda. *Current Research in Environmental Sustainability, 2,* 100017. https://doi.org/10.1016/j.crsust.2020 .100017

Gibbons, E. (2014) Climate change, children's rights, and the pursuit of inter-generational climate justice. *Health & Human Rights Journal, 16,* 19.

Gibbs, L., Block, K., Harms, L. et al. (2015). Children and young people's well-being post-disaster: Safety and stability are critical. *International Journal of Disaster Risk Reduction, 14,* 195–201. https://doi.org/10.1016/j.ijdrr.2015 .06.006

Gibbs, L., Nursey, J., Cook, J. et al. (2019). Delayed disaster impacts on academic performance of primary school children. *Child Development, 90*(4), 1402–12. https://doi.org/10.1111/cdev.13200

Gibson, K., Haslam, N., & Kaplan, I. (2019). Distressing encounters in the context of climate change: Idioms of distress, determinants, and responses to distress in Tuvalu. *Transcultural Psychiatry, 56*(4), 667–96. https://doi.org/ 10.1177/1363461519847057

Gifford, R. (2011). The dragons of inaction: Psychological barriers that limit climate change mitigation and adaptation. *American Psychologist, 66*(4), 290–302. https://doi: 10.1037/a0023566

Giusti, M., Svane, U., Raymond, C. M., & Beery, T. H. (2018). A framework to assess where and how children connect to nature. *Frontiers in Psychology, 8*, 2283. https://doi.org/10.3389/fpsyg.2017.02283

Global Action Plan UK & Unilever. (2021). *Generation action: How to unleash the potential of children and young people to take positive action and create a better world for all.* Global Action Plan UK. www.globalactionplan.org.uk/files/generation_action_white_paper.pdf

Godden, N. J., Farrant, B. M., Yallup Farrant, J. et al. (2021). Climate change, activism, and supporting the mental health of children and young people: Perspectives from Western Australia. *Journal of Paediatrics and Child Health, 57*(11), 1759–64. https://doi.org/10.1111/jpc.15649

Gottman, J., & Declaire, J. (1998). *Raising an emotionally intelligent child: The heart of parenting.* (1st ed.) Fireside.

Goumandakoye, M., & Munang, R. (2014). Engaging children in African climate change discourse. In UNICEF (Ed.), *The challenges of climate change: Children on the front line.* (Innocenti Insight). (pp. 72–4). UNICEF Office of Research – Innocenti.

Gray, E. (20 August 2018) Unexpected future boost of methane possible from Arctic permafrost. NASA. www.nasa.gov/feature/goddard/2018/unexpected-future-boost-of-methane-possible-from-arctic-permafrost

Green, C. (2018) *Children's environmental identity development: Negotiating inner and outer tensions in natural world socialization.* Peter Lang Incorporated, International Academic

Grumbach, E. (2019). From facts to solutions. *Science and Children, 56*(5), 34–41.

Guarcello, L., Mealli, F., & Rosati, F. C. (2010). Household vulnerability and child labor: The effect of shocks, credit rationing, and insurance. *Journal of Population Economics, 23*(1), 169–98.

Hahn, E. R. (2021). The developmental roots of environmental stewardship: Childhood and the climate change crisis. *Current Opinion in Psychology, 42*, 19–24. https://doi.org/10.1016/j.copsyc.2021.01.006

Hanna, R., & Oliva, P. (2016). Implications of climate change for children in developing countries. *The Future of Children, 26*(1), 115–32. https://doi.org/10.1353/foc.2016.0006

Harker-Schuch, I., Lade, S., Mills, F., & Colvin, R. (2021). Opinions of 12 to 13-year-olds in Austria and Australia on the concern, cause and imminence of climate change. *Ambio, 50*(3), 644–60. https://doi.org/10.1007/s13280-020-01356-2

Harris, K., & Hawrylyshyn, K. (2012). *Climate extremes and child rights in South Asia: A neglected priority*. Project Briefing, 78. Overseas Development Institute.

Harris, P. L. (2012). *Trusting what you're told: How children learn from others*. Harvard University Press.

Hart, R., Fisher, S., & Kimiagar, B. (2014). Beyond projects: Involving children in community governance as a fundamental strategy for facing climate change. In UNICEF Office of Research (Ed.), *The challenges of climate change: Children on the front line* (pp. 92–7). Florence: UNICEF.

Harville, E. W., Taylor, C. A., Tesfai, H., Xiong, X., & Buekens, P. (2011). Experience of Hurricane Katrina and reported intimate partner violence. *Journal of Interpersonal Violence, 26*(4), 833–45.

Hawkins, M. T., Letcher, P., Sanson, A., Smart, D., & Toumbourou, J. W. (2009). Positive development in emerging adulthood. *Australian Journal of Psychology, 61*(2), 89–99. https://doi.org/10.1080/00049530802001346

Hickman, C., Marks, E., Pihkala, P. et al. (2021). Young people's voices on climate anxiety, government betrayal and moral injury: A global phenomenon. *Lancet Planetary Health, 5*(12), e863–e873. https://doi.org/10.1016/S2542-5196(21)00278-3.

Hobfoll, S. E., Watson, P., Bell, C. C. et al. (2007). Five essential elements of immediate and mid-term mass trauma intervention: Empirical evidence. *Psychiatry, 70*(4), 283–315. https://doi.org/10.1521/psyc.2007.70.4.283

Hossain, S. (2020). Salinity and miscarriage: Is there a link? Impact of climate change in coastal areas of Bangladesh – a systematic review. *European Journal of Environment and Public Health, 4*(1), em0036. https://doi.org/10.29333/ejeph/6291

Ingle, H. E., & Mikulewicz, M. (2020). Mental health and climate change: Tackling invisible injustice. *The Lancet Planetary Health, 4*(4), e128–e130. https://doi.org/10.1016/S2542-5196(20)30081-4

Intergovernmental Panel on Climate Change. (3 November 2021). *Sixth Assessment Report: AR6 Climate Change 2021. The Physical Science Basis*. www.ipcc.ch/report/ar6/wg1/

Intergovernmental Science-Policy Platform on Biodiversity and Ecosystem Services. (2019). *Nature's dangerous decline 'unprecedented:' Species extinction rates 'accelerating.'* [Press release]. www.ipbes.net/news/Media-Release-Global-Assessment

International Labour Office & United Nations Children's Fund. (2021). *Child labour: Global estimates* 2020, *trends and the road forward*. ILO www.ilo.org/ipec/Informationresources/WCMS_797515/lang–en/index.htm

Kagawa, F., & Selby, D. (2010). Introduction. In F. Kagawa & D. Selby (Eds.), *Education and climate change: Living and learning in interesting times* (pp. 1–11). Routledge.

Karpudewan, M., Roth, W.-M., & Abdullah, M. N. S. B. (2015). Enhancing primary school students' knowledge about global warming and environmental attitude using climate change activities. *International Journal of Science Education, 37*(1), 31–54. https://doi.org/10.1080/09500693.2014 .958600

Kielland, A., & Kebede, T. A. (2020). Drought vulnerability and child mobility in rural Senegal. *Forum for Development Studies, 47*(3), 1–19, 427–45. https://doi.org/10.1080/08039410.2020.1739122

Krishna, R. N., Majeed, S., Ronan, K., & Alisic, E. (2018). Coping with disasters while living in poverty: A systematic review. *Journal of Loss and Trauma: Adversity in the Asia Pacific Region: Challenges Facing Health and Society, 23*(5), 419–38. https://doi.org/10.1080/15325024.2017 .1415724

Krishna, R. N., Ronan, K. R., & Alisic, E. (2018). Children in the 2015 South Indian floods: Community members' views. *European Journal of Psychotraumatology: Children and Disasters, 9*(Suppl 2), 1486122–11. https:// doi.org/10.1080/20008198.2018.1486122

Kulig, J. C., & Dabravolskaj, J. (2020). The psychosocial impacts of wildland fires on children, adolescents and family functioning: A scoping review. *International Journal of Wildland Fire, 29*(2), 93–103.

Kulig, J. C., Townshend, I., Botey, A. P., & Shepard, B (2018). 'Hope is in our hands': Impacts of the Slave Lake wildfires in Alberta, Canada on children. In J. Szente (Ed.), *Assisting young children caught in disasters. Educating the young child (Advances in Theory and Research, Implications for Practice)* (Vol. 13, pp. 143–56.). Springer-Cham.

Kumar, S., Molitor, R., & Vollmer, S. (2016). Drought and early child health in rural India. *Population and Development Review, 41*(1), 53–68.

Lai, B. S., Osborne, M. C., Piscitello, J., Self-Brown, S., & Kelley, M. L. (2018). The relationship between social support and posttraumatic stress symptoms among youth exposed to a natural disaster. *European Journal of Psychotraumatology, 9*(Suppl 2), 1450042. https://doi.org/10.1080/2000 8198.2018.1450042

Landis-Hanley, J. (25 October 2021). Young Australians lodge human rights complaints with UN over alleged government inaction on climate. *The Guardian.* www.theguardian.com/australia-news/2021/oct/25/young-australians-lodge-human-rights-complaints-with-un-over-alleged-government-inaction-on-climate

Lawson, D. F., Stevenson, K. T., Peterson, M. N. et al. (2019). Children can foster climate change concern among their parents. *Nature Climate Change, 9*(6), 458–62. https://doi.org/10.1038/s41558-019-0463-3

Lawton, G. (11 October 2019). Labeling eco-anxiety as 'an illness' means climate denialists have won. https://coffscoastoutlook.com.au/labeling-eco-anxiety-as-an-illness-means-climate-denialists-have-won/

Lazarus, R., & Folkman, S. (1984) *Stress, appraisal, and coping.* Springer.

Lee, K., & Barnett, J. (2020). 'Will polar bears melt?' A qualitative analysis of children's questions about climate change. *Public Understanding of Science, 29*(8), 868–80. https://doi.org/10.1177/0963662520952999

Lee, K., Gjersoe, N., O'Neill, S., & Barnett, J. (2020). Youth perceptions of climate change: A narrative synthesis. *WIREs Climate Change, 11*(3), e641. https://doi.org/10.1002/wcc.641

Leleto, N. L., & Rehse, E. (2021). How climate change affects pregnancy and early childhood in an indigenous Kenyan village. In Bernard van Leer Foundation (Ed.), *Early Childhood Matters: The Climate Issue. Caring for children and the planet.* (pp. 45–7). Bernard van Leer Foundation.

Leppold, C., Gibbs, L., Block, K., Reifels, L., & Quinn, P. (2022). Public health implications of multiple disaster exposures. *The Lancet Public Health, 7*(3), e274–e286, https://doi.org/10.1016/S2468-2667(21)00255-3

Lerner, R. M., Almerigi, J. B., & Lerner, J. V. (2005). Positive youth development A view of the issues. *The Journal of Early Adolescence, 25*(1), 10–16. https://doi.org/10.1177/0272431604273211

Louv, R. (2021). There are huge risks in raising children under what amounts to protective house arrest. In Bernard van Leer Foundation (Ed.), *Early childhood matters: The climate issue. Caring for children and the planet.* (pp. 72–4). Bernard van Leer Foundation.

MacDonald, J. P., Cunsolo Willox, A., Ford, J. D. et al. (2015). Protective factors for mental health and well-being in a changing climate: Perspectives from Inuit youth in Nunatsiavut, Labrador. *Social Science & Medicine, 141*, 133–41. https://doi.org/10.1016/j.socscimed.2015.07.017

Macy, J., & Johnstone, C. (2012). *Active hope: How to face the mess we're in without going crazy.* World Library. https://ebookcentral.proquest.com/lib/gbv/detail.action?docID=5840728.

Marazziti, D., Cianconi, P., Mucci, F. et al. (2021). Climate change, environment pollution, COVID-19 pandemic and mental health. *The Science of the Total Environment, 773*, 145182. https://doi.org/10.1016/j.scitotenv.2021.145182

Marin, A., & Bang, M. (2018). 'Look it, this is how you know': Family forest walks as a context for knowledge-building about the natural world. *Cognition and Instruction, 36*(2), 89–118. https://doi.org/10.1080/07370008.2018.1429443

Martinez, K. G. (2020). Climate change and hurricanes: The effect of hurricane-related stress on infant temperament. *Journal of the American Academy of Child & Adolescent Psychiatry, 59*(10), S39–S39. https://doi.org/10.1016/j.jaac.2020.07.163

Masten, A. S. (2014). *Ordinary magic: Resilience in development.* Guilford Press.

Masten, A. S. (2018). Schools nurture resilience of children and societies. *Green Schools Catalyst Quarterly, 3*(3), 14–19.

Masten, A. S. (2021). Resilience in developmental systems. In A. S. Masten (Ed.), *Multisystemic resilience* (pp. 113-34). Oxford University Press.

Masten, A. S., & Cicchetti, D. (2016). Resilience in development: Progress and transformation. In D. Cicchetti (Ed.), *Developmental psychopathology* (3rd Ed., pp. 271–333). Wiley.

Maternowska, M. C., Potts, A., Fry, D., & Casey, T (2018). *Research that drives change: Conceptualizing and conducting nationally led violence prevention research. Synthesis report of the 'Multi-Country Study on the Drivers of Violence Affecting Children' in Italy, Peru, Viet Nam and Zimbabwe.* UNICEF Office of Research – Innocenti.

McDonald-Harker, C., Bassi, E. M., & Haney, T. J. (2022). 'We need to do something about this': Children's and youth's post-disaster views on climate change and environmental crisis. *Sociological Inquiry, 92*(1), 5–33. https://doi.org/10.1111/soin.12381

McMichael, A. (2014). Climate change and children: Health risks of abatement inaction, health gains from action. *Children, 1,* 99–106.

Milman, O. (2021). Rising heat poses dire risks to small children. In Bernard van Leer Foundation (Ed.), *Early Childhood Matters: The climate issue. Caring for children and the planet* (pp. 31–3). Bernard van Leer Foundation.

Molina, O., & Saldarriaga, V. (2017). The perils of climate change: In utero exposure to temperature variability and birth outcomes in the Andean region. *Economics and Human Biology, 24,* 111–24. https://doi.org/10.1016/j.ehb.2016.11.009

Monroe, M. C., Plate, R. R., Oxarart, A., Bowers, A., & Chaves, W. A. (2019). Identifying effective climate change education strategies: A systematic review of the research. *Environmental Education Research, 25*(6), 791–812. https://doi.org/10.1080/13504622.2017.1360842

Morais, D. B., & Ogden, A. C. (2011). Initial development and validation of the Global Citizenship Scale. *Journal of Studies in International Education, 15*(5), 445–66. https://doi.org/10.1177/1028315310375308

Muhirwa, F. (2020). *Environmental education profile in Rwanda.* Huye-Uganda Protestant Institute of Arts and Social Sciences, Department of Natural Resources and Environmental Management.

Naylor, K. A. (2021). Climate change-induced water insecurity endangers children. In Bernard Van Leer Foundation (Ed.), *Early Childhood Matters: The climate issue. Caring for children and the planet*, (pp. 14–17). Bernard van Leer Foundation.

Newell, P., Daley, F., & Twena, M. (2022). Changing our ways: Behaviour change and the climate crisis. *Elements in Earth system governance*. Cambridge University Press.

Ochieng, M. A., & Koske, J. (2013). The level of climate change awareness and perception among primary school teachers in Kisumu municipality, Kenya. *International Journal of Humanities and Social Science, 3*(21), 174–9.

O'Connor, M., Sanson, A., Hawkins, M. T. et al. (2011). Predictors of positive development in emerging adulthood. *Journal of Youth and Adolescence, 40*(7), 860–74. https://doi.org/10.1007/s10964-010-9593-7

Ojala, M. (2012a). How do children cope with global climate change? Coping strategies, engagement, and well-being. *Journal of Environmental Psychology, 32*(3), 225–33. https://doi.org/10.1016/j.jenvp.2012.02.004

Ojala, M. (2012b). Regulating worry, promoting hope: How do children, adolescents, and young adults cope with climate change? *International Journal of Environmental and Science Education, 7*(4), 537–61.

Ojala, M. (2013). Coping with climate change among adolescents: Implications for subjective wellbeing and environmental engagement. *Sustainability* 5 (5), 2191–209. https://doi.org/10.3390/su5052191.

Ojala, M. (2015). Hope in the face of climate change: Associations with environmental engagement and student perceptions of teachers' emotion communication style and future orientation. *The Journal of Environmental Education, 46*(3), 133–48.

Ojala, M. (2016a). Preparing children for the emotional challenges of climate change: A review of the research. In K. Winograd (Ed.), *Education in times of environmental crises* (pp. 210–8). Routledge.

Ojala, M. (2016b). Young people and global climate change: Emotions, coping, and engagement in everyday life. In N. Ansell, N. Klocker & T. Skelton (Eds.), *Geographies of global issues: Change and threat: Geographies of children and young people* (pp. 1–19). Springer Science + Business Media.

Ojala, M. (2021). Commentary: Climate change worry among adolescents – On the importance of going beyond the constructive-unconstructive dichotomy to explore coping efforts – a commentary on Sciberras and Fernando (2021). *Child and Adolescent Mental Health, 27*(1), 89–91. https://doi.org/10.1111/camh.12530

Ojala, M., & Bengtsson, H. (2019). Young people's coping strategies concerning climate change: Relations to perceived communication with parents and friends and pro environmental behavior. *Environment and Behavior*, *51*(8), pp. 907–35. https://doi.org/10.1177/00139165187 63894

Otto, S., & Pensini, P. (2017). Nature-based environmental education of children: Environmental knowledge and connectedness to nature, together, are related to ecological behaviour. *Global Environmental Change*, 47, pp. 88–94. https://doi.org/10.1016/j.gloenvcha.2017.09.009

Otto, S., Evans, G. W., Moon, M. J., & Kaiser, F. G. (2019). The development of children's environmental attitude and behavior. *Global Environmental Change*, *58*, 101947. https://doi.org/10.1016/j.gloenvcha.2019.101947

Our Children's Trust. (2018). *Colombia. Demanda generaciones futuras.* MINAMBIENTE. www.ourchildrenstrust.org/colombia-global-summary.

Pacheco, S. E. (2020). Catastrophic effects of climate change on children's health start before birth. *The Journal of Clinical Investigation*, *130*(2), 562–4. https://doi.org/10.1172/JCI135005

Padilla, K., & Bernheim, R. (2020). *Act now: Experiences and recommendations of girls and boys during COVID-19.* World Vision International. www .wvi.org/publications/report/coronavirus-health-crisis/act-now-experiences-and-recommendations-girls-and-0

Peek, L., Abramson, D. M., Cox, R. S., Fothergill, A., & Tobin, J. (2018). Children and disasters. In H. Rodríguez, W. Donner, & J. E. Trainor (Eds.), *Handbook of Disaster Research*, (2nd Ed., pp. 243–62). Springer.

Pereznieto, P., Rivett, J., Le Masson, V., George, R., & Marcurs, R. (2020). *Ending violence against children while addressing the global climate crisis.* World Vision International. https://odi.org/en/publications/ending-violence-against-children-while-addressing-the-global-climate-crisis/.

Petersen, A. C., Koller, S. H., Motti-Stefandi, F., & Verma, S. (2017). *Positive youth development in global contexts of social and economic change.* Routledge.

Pfefferbaum, B., Varma, V., Nitiéma, P., & Newman, E. (2014). Universal preventive interventions for children in the context of disasters and terrorism. *Child and Adolescent Psychiatric Clinics of North America*, *23*(2), 363–82, ix–x. https://doi.org/10.1016/j.chc.2013.12.006

Pihkala, P. (2020). Eco-anxiety and environmental education. *Sustainability*, *12*(23), 10149. https://doi.org/10.3390/su122310149

Polack, E. (2010). *Child rights and climate change adaptation: Voices from Kenya and Cambodia.* Institute of Development Studies, Plan International. https://resourcecentre.savethechildren.net/document/child-rights-and-climate-change-adaptation-voices-kenya-and-cambodia/

Putnick, D. L., & Bornstein, M. H. (2016). Girls' and boys' labor and household chores in low- and middle-income countries. *Monograph of the Society for Research in Child Development, 81,* 104–22. https://doi.org/10.1111/mono .12228

Reid, A. (2019). Climate change education and research: Possibilities and potentials versus problems and perils? *Environmental Education Research, 25*(6), 767–90. https://doi.org/10.1080/13504622.2019.1664075

Rello, R. L., & Ackers, J. (2020). *Rising to the challenge: Youth perspectives on climate change and education in South Asia.* UNICEF. www.unicef.org/rosa/ reports/rising-challenge

Ronan, K. R., & Jhonston, D. M. (2005). *Promoting community resilience in disasters the role for schools, youth, and families.* Springer.

Rousell, D., & Cutter-Mackenzie-Knowles, A. (2019). A systematic review of climate change education: Giving children and young people a 'voice' and a 'hand' in redressing climate change. *Children's Geographies, 18*(2), 191–208. https://doi.org/10.1080/14733285.2019.1614532

Rubenstein, B. L., & Stark, L. (2017). The impact of humanitarian emergencies on the prevalence of violence against children: An evidence-based ecological framework. *Psychology, Health & Medicine, 22*(sup1), 58–66. https://doi .org/10.1080/13548506.2016.1271949

Sanson, A., & Bellemo, M. (2021). Children and youth in the climate crisis. *BJPsych Bulletin, 45*(4), 205–9. https://doi.org/10.1192/bjb.2021.16

Sanson, A., Wachs, T. D., Koller, S. H., & Salmela-Aro, K. (2018). Young people and climate change: The role of developmental science. In S. Verma, S. & A. C. Petersen (Eds.), *Developmental science and sustainable development goals for children and youth.* Social Indicators Research Series, 74 (pp. 115–38). Springer.

Sanson, A. V., & Burke, S. (2019). Climate change and children: An issue of intergenerational justice. In N. Balvin & D. J. Christie (Eds.), *Children and peace: From research to action* (pp. 343–62). Springer.

Sanson, A. V., Burke, S., & Van Hoorn, J. (2018). Climate change: Implications for parents and parenting. *Parenting, 18*(3), 200–17. https://doi.org/10.1080/ 15295192.2018.1465307

Sanson, A. V., Padilla Malca, K. V., & Van Hoorn, J. (2022). Impact of the climate crisis on children's social development. In P. K. Smith, & Hart, C. H. (Eds.), *The Wiley-Blackwell handbook of childhood social development,* 3rd Ed. (pp. 206–23). Wiley.

Sanson, A. V., Van Hoorn, J., & Burke, S. (2019). Responding to the impacts of the climate crisis on children and youth. *Child Development Perspectives, 13*(4), 201–7. https://doi.org/10.1111/cdep.12342

Schoon, I. (2021). A sociological development systems approach for the study of human resilience. In M. Ungar (Ed.), *Multisystemic resilience. Processes in research and practice: Adaptation and transformation in contexts of change* (pp. 335–60). Oxford University Press.

Scott, B. G., Lapré, G. E., Marsee, M. A., & Weems, C. F (2014). Aggressive behavior and its associations with posttraumatic stress and academic achievement following a natural disaster. *Journal of Clinical Child and Adolescent Psychology, 43*(1), 43–50. https://doi.org/10.1080/15374416.2013.807733

Shinn, L. (2019). *Your guide to talking with kids of all ages about climate change.* www.nrdc.org/stories/your-guide-talking-kids-all-ages-about-climate-change

Skanavis, C., & Kounani, A. (2018). Children communicating on climate change: The case of a summer camp at a Greek island. In W. Leal Filho, E. Manolas, A. M. Azul, U. M. Azeiteiro, & H. McGhie (Eds.), *Handbook of climate change communication* (Vol. 3, pp. 113–130). Springer. https://doi.org/10.1007/978-3-319-70479-1_7

Sobel, D. (2008). *Children and nature.* Stenhouse Books.

Songok, C. K., Kipkorir, E. C., Mugalavai, E. M., Kwonyike, A. C., & Ng'weno, C. (2011). Improving the participation of agro-pastoralists in climate change adaptation and disaster risk reduction policy formulation: A case study from Keiyo district, Kenya. In W. Leal Filho (Ed.), *Experiences of climate change adaptation in Africa* (pp. 55–68). Springer.

Steffen, W., Fenwick, J., & Rice, M. (2018). Trajectories of the earth system in the Anthropocene. *Proceedings of the National Academy of Sciences of the United States of America, 115*(33), 8252–9. https://doi.org/10.1073/pnas.1810141115

Steffen, W., Fenwick, J., & Rice, M. (2016). *Land carbon: No substitute for action on fossil fuels.* Climate Council of Australia. www.climatecouncil.org.au/uploads/aadc6ea123523a46102e2be45bfcedc8.pdf

Stevenson, K., & Peterson, N. (2016). Motivating action through fostering climate change hope and concern and avoiding despair among adolescents. *Sustainability, 8*(1), 6. https://doi.org/10.3390/su8010006

Stough, L. M., Ducy, E. M., & Kang, D. (2017). Addressing the needs of children with disabilities experiencing disaster or terrorism. *Current Psychiatry Reports, 19*(4), p. 1.

Swaminathan, A., Lucas, R. M., Harley, D., & McMichael, A. J. (2014). Will global climate change alter fundamental human immune reactivity: Implications for child health? *Children, 1*(3), 403–23. https://doi.org/10.3390/children1030403

Taylor, M., Watts, J., & Bartlett, J. (27 September 2019). Climate crisis: 6 million people join latest wave of global protests. *The Guardian.* www.theguardian.com/environment/2019/sep/27/climate-crisis-6-million-people-join-latest-wave-of-worldwide-protests.

Thiery, W., Lange, S., Rogelj, J. et al. (2021). Intergenerational inequities in exposure to climate extremes. *Science, 374*(6564), 158–60. https://doi.org/10.1126/science.abi7339

Tillmann, S., Tobin, D., Avison, W., & Gilliland, J. (2018). Mental health benefits of interactions with nature in children and teenagers: A systematic review. *Journal of Epidemiological Community Health, 72*, pp. 958–66. https://doi.org/10.1136/jech-2018-210436

Towers, B., Christianson, A. C., & Eriksen, C. (2020). Impacts of wildfire on children. In S. L. Manzello (Ed.), *Encyclopedia of wildfires and wildland-urban interface (WUI) fires* (pp. 684–92). Springer.

Trombley, J., Chalupka, S., & Anderko, L. (2017). Climate change and mental health. *The American Journal of Nursing, 117*(4), 44–52. https://doi.org/10.1097/01.NAJ.0000515232.51795.fa

Trott, C. D. (2019). Reshaping our world: Collaborating with children for community-based climate change action. *Action Research, 17*(1), 42–62. https://doi.org/10.1177/1476750319829209

Tudge, J. R. H. (2008). *The everyday lives of young children: Culture, class, and child rearing in diverse societies.* Cambridge University Press.

United Nations. (1989). *Convention on the rights of the child. United Nations Treaty Series, 1577*(3). https://www.ohchr.org/en/instruments-mechanisms/instruments/convention-rights-child

United Nations. (9 August 2021). *Guterres: The IPCC Report is a code red for humanity* [Press release]. www.un.org/press/en/2021/sgsm20847.doc.htm

United Nations CC: Learn. (2013). *Resource guide for advanced learning on: Integrating climate change in education at primary and secondary level.* www.uncclearn.org/wp-content/uploads/library/resource_guide_on_integrating_cc_in_education_primary_and_secondary_level.pdf.

United Nations Educational, Scientific, and Cultural Organization. (2021). *Learn for our planet: A global review of how environmental issues are integrated into education.* Paris UNESCO (Education 2030). https://unesdoc.unesco.org/ark:/48223/pf0000377362.

United Nations Children's Fund. (2014). *The challenges of climate change: Children on the front line.* Florence: UNICEF Office of Research. www.unicef-irc.org/publications/716-the-challenges-of-climate-change-children-on-the-front-line.html

United Nations Children's Fund. (2021a). *The climate crisis is a child rights crisis. Introducing the Children's Climate Risk Index.* https://www.unicef.org/reports/climate-crisis-child-rights-crisis

United Nations Children's Fund. (18 August 2021b). *UNICEF Executive Director Henrietta Fore's remarks at the launch of UNICEF's first child-focused climate risk index with Greta Thunberg and other youth activists* [Press release]. www.unicef.org/press-releases/unicef-executive-director-henrietta-fores-remarks-launch-unicefs-first-child-focused United Nations Children's Fund. (20 January 2021c). *Normal life washed away in Guatemala.* https://www.unicef.org/lac/en/stories/normal-life-washed-away-in-guatemala

United Nations Children's Fund, United Nations Major Group for Children and Youth, World Vision International, Plan International, & Save the Children. (2020). *Guardians of the planet: Asia Pacific children and youth voices on climate crisis and disaster risk reduction.* UNICEF East Asia and Pacific Regional Office.

United Nations News. (25 January 2019). *Climate change recognized as 'threat multiplier', UN Security Council debates its impact on peace.* https://news.un.org/en/story/2019/01/1031322

United Nations News. (31 March 2020). U*N launches COVID-19 plan that could 'defeat the virus and build a better world'.* https://news.un.org/en/story/2020/03/1060702.

United Nations Secretary General. (31 March 2020). Opening remarks at virtual press encounter to launch the Report on the Socio-Economic Impacts of COVID-19. United Nations Secretary-General [Press release]. www.un.org/sg/en/content/sg/speeches/2020-03-31/remarks-launch-of-report-the-socio-economic-impacts-of-covid-19

Van Nieuwenhuizen, A., Hudson, K., Chen, X., & Hwong, A. R. (2021). The effects of climate change on child and adolescent mental health: Clinical considerations. *Current Psychiatry Reports*, *23*(12), 88. https://doi.org/10.1007/s11920-021-01296-y

Watts, J. (3 November 2020). Portuguese children sue 33 countries over climate change at European court. *The Guardian.* www.theguardian.com/law/2020/sep/03/portuguese-children-sue-33-countries-over-climate-change-at-european-court.

Wiseman, J. (2021). *Hope and courage in the climate crisis: Wisdom and action in the long emergency.* Springer Nature.

Wu, J., Snell, G., & Samji, H. (2020). Climate anxiety in young people: A call to action. *The Lancet Planetary Health*, *4*(10), e435–e436. https://doi.org/10.1016/S2542-5196(20)30223-0

Yelland, C., Robinson, P., Lock, C. et al. (2010). Bushfire impact on youth. *Journal of Traumatic Stress*, *23*(2), 274–7. https://doi.org/10.1002/jts.20521

Cambridge Elements ☰

Child Development

Marc H. Bornstein

Eunice Kennedy Shriver National Institute of Child Health and Human Development, Bethesda

Institute for Fiscal Studies, London

UNICEF, New York City

Marc H. Bornstein is an Affiliate of the *Eunice Kennedy Shriver* National Institute of Child Health and Human Development, an International Research Fellow at the Institute for Fiscal Studies (London), and UNICEF Senior Advisor for Research for ECD Parenting Programmes. Bornstein is President Emeritus of the Society for Research in Child Development, Editor Emeritus of *Child Development*, and founding Editor of *Parenting: Science and Practice*.

About the Series

Child development is a lively and engaging, yet serious and real-world subject of scientific study that encompasses myriad theories, methods, substantive areas, and applied concerns. Cambridge Elements in Child Development addresses many contemporary topics in child development with unique, comprehensive, and state-of-the-art treatments of principal issues, primary currents of thinking, original perspectives, and empirical contributions to understanding early human development.

Cambridge Elements ≡

Child Development

Elements in the Series

Printed in the United States
by Baker & Taylor Publisher Services